Flanders Lace
A step-by-step guide

Mary Niven

Dryad Press Ltd London

Flanders Lace

This book is dedicated firstly to the memory of my father, the late Dr F. E. Woodthorpe, whose enthusiasm for making lace bobbins started me on the road to lacemaking. Secondly it is dedicated to all those hundreds of lacemakers who laboured long and difficult hours for small reward, to give us such a rich heritage of exquisite beauty and workmanship. Long may we treasure, respect and admire their labours.

Acknowledgments

I wish to thank all those kind people who have both directly and indirectly contributed their guidance, help and encouragement to the production of this book. In particular I wish to thank Mvr Ghislaine Moors, Mrs Tordis Berendt, Mme Remy, Mr Van Dongen, Mrs Elaine Merrit, Mvr Diane Claeys, Mme Ghyslaine Maes.

© Mary Niven 1988
First published 1988

Typeset by Tek-Art Ltd, Kent
and printed by Colorcraft Ltd,
Hong Kong
for the publishers,
Dryad Press Ltd,
8 Cavendish Square,
London W1M 0AJ

ISBN 0 8521 9691 1

Contents

Preface

1 Introduction   8

2 Equipment   10

3 The Flanders ground   20

4 The pea motifs   27

5 The corner   36

6 Chevrons and wavy edges
                                                    43

7 Holes and straight-line
   beginning and finishing
   of cloth stitch areas   54

8 The double-pointed
   corner   64

9 Fillings   73

10 More advanced patterns   88

Glossary   110

Suppliers   113

Index   115

Grids   117

Preface

This book is intended as a first introduction to Flanders lace, covering all the basic and important technical features found in patterns both in general circulation and in this book.

To simplify the learning process, and also for quick reference, these techniques have been divided into chapters beginning with the basic principles and progressing to the more involved methods. In this way the book can be used as a teach-yourself or class-teaching guide, as well as a reference book for those who may have already worked some Flanders lace.

Chapters 3-7 and 9 are divided into three sections. The first deals with the historical aspects of the techniques covered in the chapter (this can be omitted by the beginner).

The second section covers the technical points of Flanders lace relevant to the chapter. Where appropriate, diagrams of a technique in the Belgian colour-coding system are accompanied by a line-drawing of the same technique (as a black line-drawing showing the individual thread movements). This is to help those who are unfamiliar with the use of colour-coded diagrams. (See Chapter 2 for a full explanation of the Belgian colour-coding system and guidance on the diagrams found in this book.)

The third section contains patterns which make use of the techniques explained in the chapter. These patterns become more advanced as the book progresses.

All patterns are accompanied by working diagrams. As it is not always necessary for the entire diagram to be in colour, sometimes only special watchpoints are coloured and the rest of the diagram left as a black line-drawing.

At the back of the book there is a glossary of terms in English, Flemish, French, and Danish.

1

Introduction

In order to understand the development of lacemaking from the beginning of the seventeenth century in the area now called Belgium, it is helpful to know a little of that country's history. It covers what was once the trade crossroads of Europe, and has been responsible for producing some of the world's most beautiful bobbin laces, despite its often traumatic past. It has been beset by wars, with all the turmoil inflicted by invading armies; it has undergone financial depression; and it has been governed by several different countries and influenced by the cultures of Spain, Austria, and France. There were two key factors behind the success of the Flemish lace industry. The first of these was the shrewd business acumen of the designers and sellers of the lace who adapted quickly to the ever-changing demands of fashionable European court society. The second was the land itself, which was perfect for producing the best quality linen threads with which to make the finest laces.

The name Flanders tends to be used to refer to two styles of lace. First the Old Flanders (see Chapter 2) which began by using torchon, then the early five-hole ground, was made in the Antwerp area which was then part of the Spanish Netherlands. The five-hole ground continued to be used by lacemakers in other areas, after they had moved away from the main centre at Antwerp, in towns such as Mechelen, Gent, Valencienne (France), and Binche. The style of lace known as Binche had a separate yet parallel development, and has many similarities in style and technique which result from copying and the demands of fashion.

Today, the term Flanders lace is more usually applied to a late-nineteenth-century revival of the five-hole grounded lace. This revival was paralled by a revival of Binche lace, which was re-named 'Fairy-Point' for commercial reasons.

In some cases of Flanders lace, many of the old techniques were not revived, and some, as can be seen from the historical notes at the beginning of each chapter, were changed. As well as use of generally coarser threads, cotton instead of linen, a new feature was incorporated – the heavier outlining gimp thread which runs around the outside of the cloth stitch areas to clearly define the design. In addition, the motifs were simplified, probably because of commercial pressures. It is interesting to note that the laces with the five-hole ground have lasted well and proved to be very practical and durable, while still leaving a great deal of scope for design and development.

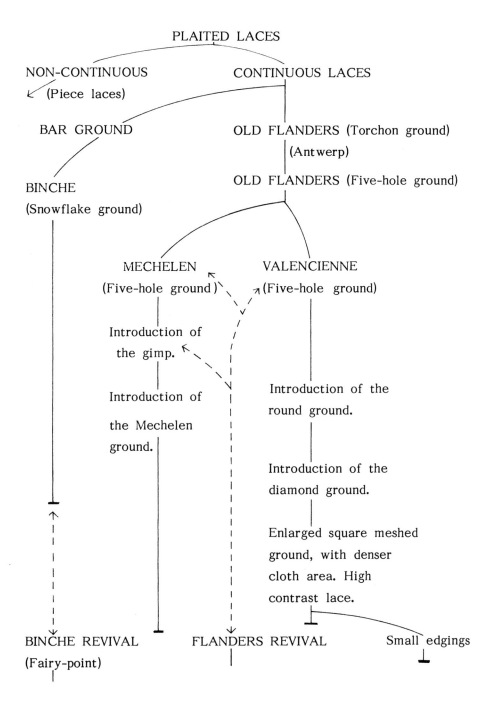

PLAITED LACES

NON-CONTINUOUS
(Piece laces)

CONTINUOUS LACES

BAR GROUND

OLD FLANDERS (Torchon ground)

(Antwerp)

BINCHE
(Snowflake ground)

OLD FLANDERS (Five-hole ground)

MECHELEN
(Five-hole ground)

VALENCIENNE
(Five-hole ground)

Introduction of
the gimp.

Introduction of
the Mechelen
ground.

Introduction of the
round ground.

Introduction of the
diamond ground.

Enlarged square meshed
ground, with denser
cloth area. High
contrast lace.

BINCHE REVIVAL
(Fairy-point)

FLANDERS REVIVAL

Small edgings

DIAGRAM 1. *The basic stylistic developments of the continuous bobbin laces made in, and close to the area now called Belgium between 1500 and 1950. To retain clarity it has been necessary to simplify the lines of development by omitting small offshoots and influences. The diagram relates purely to the commercial production of the lace.*

9

2

Equipment

Modern and traditional Flanders lacemaking equipment: stands, pillows, bobbins, threads, long and short pins, the pricking, the pattern, and the working diagram. The Belgian colour-coding system.

The tools for any craft are very important if the best results are to be obtained, and Flanders lace is no exception to this rule.

The stand

A stand is a simple, adjustable support for the lace pillow used whilst working. Stands have been used for lacemaking in Belgium for a very long time. It is not intended that these stands should carry the whole of the pillow; they act as a support for the edge of the pillow furthest away from the lap of the lacemaker. The height of the stand can be easily adjusted, thus giving a comfortable position in which to work. The lacemaker's back and neck need not be bent over at an awkward angle, and the arms can be in a more relaxed position for maximum movement and speed (see diagram 2 Figs 1a and 1b). The stand is not not a vital piece of equipment, as many other pieces of household furniture can perform the same function. The most important thing is for the height and angle of the pillow to be correct and comfortable.

The lace pillow

The style of the Old Flanders lace pillow, shown in diagram 2 Fig. 3, has remained relatively unchanged since the 1600s. If anything, the more recently made pillows are a little larger. It is not surprising that the design of this pillow has remained so popular, as it is perfectly designed and equipped for the job of making continuous straight lace.

This pillow has one or two interesting features, shown in the diagram. For example, it has a drawer in the right-hand side in which to keep bobbins, support pins, scissors, etc. It is extremely rare to find a lace pillow with a drawer on the left-hand side. This is most probably because of strong religious, or superstitious, beliefs and traditions regarding the left-hand side, which was considered bad luck or in some way connected with the devil. The top end of the pillow pulls away and has two wooden bars sticking out from it. These bars can be slotted into the two holes in the opposite side of the pillow, thus extending its working length. When the extension is removed from the top end of the pillow, it reveals another drawer which is intended to hold the finished lace (see diagram 2 Fig. 3).

The modern demand for lace pillows suitable for making circular or oval pieces as well as corners has led to the development of a variety of styles. These range from large circular to semi-circular pillows, with or without interchangeable central blocks (see diagram 2 Fig. 2).

Whichever style of pillow is preferred,

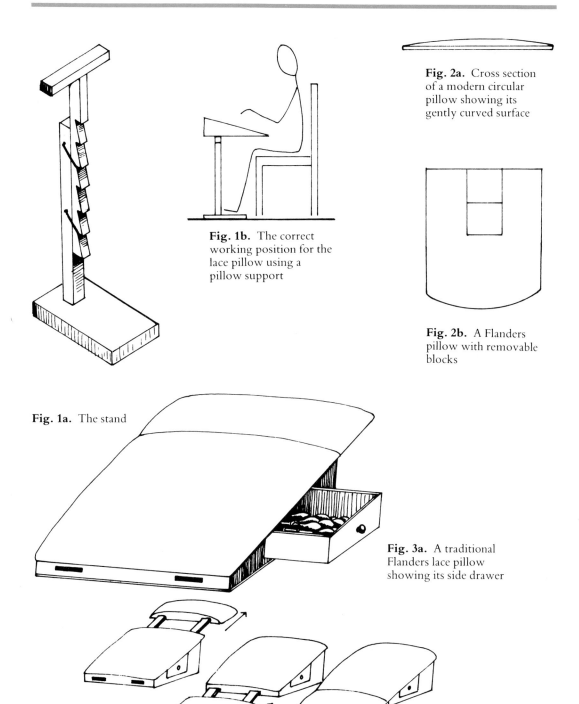

Fig. 2a. Cross section of a modern circular pillow showing its gently curved surface

Fig. 1b. The correct working position for the lace pillow using a pillow support

Fig. 2b. A Flanders pillow with removable blocks

Fig. 1a. The stand

Fig. 3a. A traditional Flanders lace pillow showing its side drawer

Fig. 3b. The use of the pillow extension

DIAGRAM 2. *Flanders lacemaking equipment*

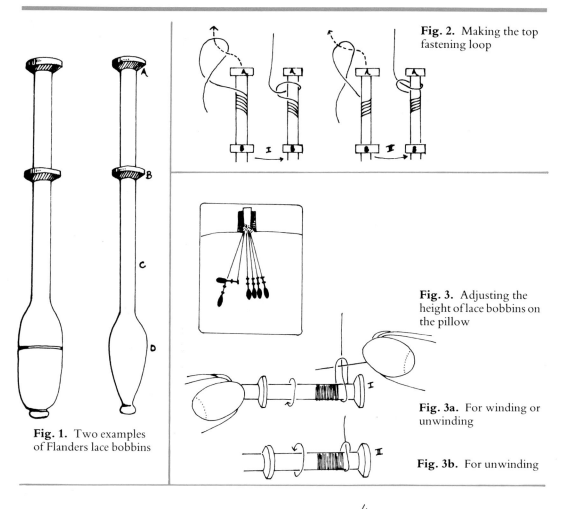

Fig. 1. Two examples of Flanders lace bobbins

Fig. 2. Making the top fastening loop

Fig. 3. Adjusting the height of lace bobbins on the pillow

Fig. 3a. For winding or unwinding

Fig. 3b. For unwinding

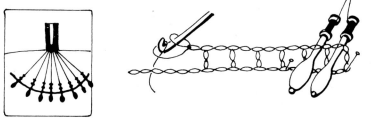

Fig. 4. The crochet loops to support the lace bobbins while moving the pillow

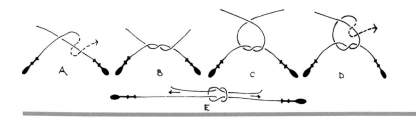

Fig. 5. The method of tying the knot on a broken thread

DIAGRAM 3.

the most important features are listed below.

1) *The depth of the pillow and its angle of slope*
(See diagram 2 Fig. 2a)
This is a particularly important feature. For example, on a standard circular pillow approximately 62 cm in diameter, the depth of the pillow at its centre should not exceed 7 cm. (This measurement includes the 1.5 cm depth of the baseboard.) The angle of the slope on the traditional pillow is lessened when placed in the working position (see diagram 2 Fig. 1b) and the working surface of the pillow has only a gentle slope from back to front and centre to sides. The necessity for a comparatively, but never exactly, flat pillow is because of the type of lace bobbins used and the techniques involved in the making of the lace itself, which require only a light tension. The steeper the slope of the pillow, the greater the tension on the threads.

The fillings for Belgian lace pillows were traditionally made from sea-grass, the tough grass that grows on the dunes along the sandy North Belgian coast. The salt on the grass kept the lace pillows 'bug-free'. Hay was also used, but it was always the first-cut hay, thus avoiding the knots and joints in the stems that hardened later in the season. Knots can prevent pins being inserted into the pillow.

2) *The firmness of the lace pillow*
If a pillow is not firm enough to keep the working pins in place once they have been inserted, the pins will not hold the threads in their correct position, and the resulting lace will not be accurate. A really firm pillow is essential for good lacemaking.

3) *The cover*
The best covering for the working surface of a Flanders lace pillow is made from close, smooth, plain-woven linen. This is because the fibres separate easily when large support pins are inserted into the pillow, and, when the pins are removed,

the fibres close back again leaving the minimum damage to the fabric. A cotton covering does not allow this movement of threads as it is of a much finer weave, and therefore the fabric would wear out far more quickly. Velvet and woollen covers are not suitable because of the small loose fibres that can separate away from the fabric and become entangled in the lace.

Many modern Belgian lace pillows are covered in a natural-coloured linen which is comfortable on the eyes, but traditionally a dark blue or green was used, as it makes the threads even easier to see. A patterned cover should not be used for Flanders lace, as it makes working difficult and confusing.

An extra cover cloth of smooth cotton, placed across the pillow with its hemmed edge about 3 cm below the working edge of the lace, is required to protect the main pillow covering from extra wear by the bobbins. This cover is also essential to smooth the passage of the threads over the underlying pattern and its holding pins, protecting the threads from wear.

The lace bobbins

A Belgian lace bobbin has some special distinctive features. For example, there is no thistle-head-shaped top as in the English Midland or French bobbins. The thread is looped around the top as in Diagram 3 Fig. 2, and wound on to the section of the bobbin between points A and B in an anticlockwise direction. (It is not important whether the bobbins are wound in a clockwise or anti-clockwise direction, and directions for making the top securing loop have been included (for both methods of winding see diagram 3 Fig. 3).

Section C of the bobbin is usually slim, swelling into a bulb shape at the end of section D, the design of which can vary according to the tastes of the lace-bobbin maker. The general rule when choosing Belgian bobbins is that, as the bulb end to the bobbin provides its weight and balance, the smaller the bulb the finer the accompanying thread should be. This weight and balance of the lace bobbin is very important when making Belgian laces. Because an even tension on the threads is also necessary, it is best to use bobbins of only one style and size at a time.

Belgian bobbins are now available in a wide range of woods and sizes. The best of these have a well-polished finish which makes them comfortable and enjoyable to handle. There are no spangles or other beads added to the base of these bobbins.

The working position of the lace bobbins and their adjustment

To facilitate easy working of the lace bobbins, it is necessary to keep their tops as level as possible when on the pillow. To adjust their height, see diagram 3 Fig. 3.

To lower the top of the bobbin, turn it sideways until it is at right angles to the other bobbins. With the thread only slightly taut, gently turn the bobbin in the direction opposite to that in which the thread was wound, until the bobbin top is level with the others. If the thread does not unwind easily, use a pin to ease the loop away from the others as in diagram 3 Fig. 3. To raise the level of the bobbin, insert a pin into the loop as shown, and loosen this 'securing loop' slightly. Keeping the pin in the loop, twist the bobbin sideways until it is at right angles to the other bobbins on the pillow and, slightly tightening the thread, turn the bobbin in the same direction as that in which the thread was wound. The bobbin will rise up the pillow. Stop when the bobbin is level with the tops of the other lace bobbins.

As far as possible the threads should not be touched by the fingers as this is a bad habit which can lead to a grey-coloured lace.

To secure lace bobbins on a lace pillow while travelling

A useful and easily-made accessory for the lace pillow is a simple and quickly made crochet chain (one treble, one chain worked back across it into every alternate basic chain as shown in diagram 3 Fig. 4). This row of crochet loops is usually made of wool as this stretches easily. If ever a large number of bobbins have to be carried in this way, make a double row of crochet loops. The bobbins are slotted through the spaces, bulb end first and in their correct working order as shown in the diagram. When all the bobbins have been inserted into the crochet chain, it can be then pinned securely to the lace pillow. The bobbins will remain held in place until they are next needed for work.

The threads

Traditionally, apart from metallic and silk, only linen thread was used for lacemaking and these threads were of course handspun. By the 1830s mechanised spinning of cotton had been developed sufficiently to enable cheaper cotton threads to be used in the lacemaking industry. By 1835 increasing quantities of lace were made using cotton thread. This encroachment by cotton was accompanied by the decline of the more labour-intensive linen industry, so that today it is impossible to purchase new linen threads of the finer counts suitable for lacemaking, and it is necessary to use cotton instead.

Different manufacturers produce different qualities of cotton thread. Unfortunately for the lacemaker, the availability of the different sizes and makes seems to be in a constant state of change, with many of the most suitable threads going completely out of production.

The best of the threads currently available are those from Egypt. They are strong, smooth, and reliable, and are available as both bleached and natural (the latter being variable in shade, often from spool to spool in the same count). Another quality of the Egyptian thread is its silky sheen, which gives extra vitality to the finished lace. Another very good and reliable thread is Brock, made in Belgium, which is available only in a bleached white.

It is important to remember when choosing threads that, even though two or three different manufacturers' threads have the same count or weight number, they may look and work up differently. This is because some are more tightly spun up than others, and so will work up like a finer-counted thread. A lightly-spun thread will have the opposite effect, and could possibly be weaker as a result. For example, the Egyptian thread count of 90/2 (which has been used for the samples of lace in this book) would be equivalent to a Brock 100/2 or 120/2.

The size of the joining thread, for sewing completed pieces of lace together, is always approximately two counts finer than that with which the lace was made – therefore Egyptian 120/2 or its equivalent is required when Egyptian 90/2 is used for the lace.

A large amount of thread of the same size can be wound on all your bobbins at one time, and this will be useful for working several patterns consecutively. This is possible because in Flanders lace (special motifs excepted), bobbins do not have to be wound into pairs to start. The *gimp thread*, (the thicker thread that sometimes outlines the areas of cloth stitch) should not be too heavy. The choice of size is a matter of personal preference. A smaller outlining gimp balances well with the delicate patterns, and with most of the samples of lace in this book Brillante d'Alsace number 20 by DMC has been used. This lovely thread has now been taken off the market and the nearest thread generally available is the DMC 25 (perhaps too thick for most of the patterns in this book) or the Brock 36/3. Whichever gimp thread is chosen it should enhance, not dominate, a pattern. A mercerised thread with a shiny finish looks very pretty and is generally more attractive in the finished lace than a matt one.

Choice of thread reflects the personal taste of the lacemaker. The suggestions made here are guidelines to help in the selection of appropriate thread. If Flanders lace is made with a thread that is too heavy, the delicate effect of the pattern will be lost. At the other extreme, a thread that is too fine will not produce a wearable lace, and the cloth stitch areas may not cover well enough, leaving unsightly gaps and holes and resulting in an ill-defined pattern.

Working and support pins

Working pins
For Flanders lace, as with all the continuous laces, a long working pin is traditional. There are several reasons for this. The most important is that the pins are not pressed down completely into the pillow – in contrast to the making of piece laces such as Duchesse, Rosaline and Honiton. The pins need to be long enough to be moved easily in and out of position, while at the same time the pin heads are far enough away from the surface of the lace to allow for easy viewing of the pattern when the pins are gently pushed to one side. Another important feature of pins for continuous lace is the metal from which they are made. They must be rustproof, and have a spring-back quality if bent; hence traditional brass pins are the best. Different-sized pins are required for different-sized grounds. In this book brass pins sized 39.6 mm have been used: shorter pins may be used instead. Pins that are too wide for the pattern can leave ugly gaps in the finished lace; too fine a pin will not hold the lace securely in position while it is being made, and inaccurate lace may result.

There are many theories as to the best method of inserting the pins into the pattern and pillow as the lace is being made. Some people favour inserting the pins angled towards the back, while others favour placing them all upright and at right

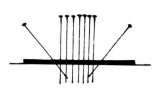

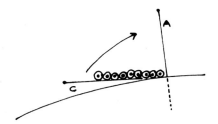

Fig. 1. Cross section of the pattern on the lace pillow, showing the working pin position from the front

Fig. 3. Collecting the bobbins in order with the second support pin

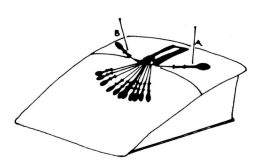

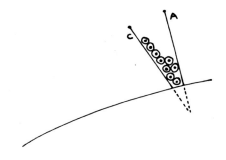

Fig. 2. The position for the first support pins

Fig. 4. Positioning the second support pin

DIAGRAM 4.

angles to the surface of the pattern. Whichever method is preferred, the aim is to keep the lace flush to the surface of the pattern, thus retaining its accuracy. If the pins are not inserted carefully, or if the lace is allowed to ride up the pins off the surface of the pattern, the result can be distorted and inaccurate. The two outside edges of the lace and the evenness of the ground are particularly important.

One method of achieving this accuracy is to angle the outside pins away from the middle of the lace (ensuring that the pins are always kept at the same angle). The pins in the main part of the lace should be at exact right angles to the surface of pattern as shown in diagram 4 Fig. 1. None of the pins slope towards the back or the front.

Supporting pins
These are traditional large brass pins approximately 17 cm long, used to hold unwanted bobbins out of the way while the others are being worked. These pins are essential when using large numbers of bobbins, allowing easier bobbin control and therefore more accurate, speedy and relaxed lacemaking.

Diagram 4 Fig. 2 shows the layout of the

lace pillow with one supporting pin in position of each side of the lace (shown at points A and B). Note that when a bobbin is moved to the side of the pillow, the supporting pin should be against the mid-point of the bobbin (see diagram). These first support pins may need to be moved down the pillow as work progresses, so that when a bobbin is pushed to the side its thread does not catch on the pins at the side of the lace or upset the tension of the threads of the side pairs.

After the first support pin (A) is securely in place, to insert the second it is necessary to slide it point end first (see fig. 3) gently under the middle of approximately 6-8 pairs of bobbins. Too large a group tends to muddle the bobbin order. Slide the point of the support pin up the pillow until it is about 1 cm away from the base of the previous pin. Carefully tilt the pin into an almost vertical position (see Fig. 4) and push it into the cushion until it is firm. As you do this, the bobbins should gently slide into the space between the two support pins; see A and C on Fig. 4. Subsequently bobbins can be piled up on either side of the pillow, one behind the other, in exactly the same manner, according to the requirements of the pattern.

To regain the correct order of the bobbins, carefully reverse the process. If the gap between the bases of pins A and C on Fig. 4 has not been too wide, and not too many bobbins have been placed in between the support pins, the recovered order of bobbins should be correct. Always check over the order of the threads before working them, just to make sure that no mistake has been made.

The pattern and the pricking

Originally, patterns and prickings were made by men as a profession separate from that of the lacemaker; these patterns were passed on to lacemakers according to their skill. A sample of lace was first made by a very experienced lacemaker; pieces of this were then passed around to other less skilled lacemakers, together with the new pattern, for them to copy. At the time, this was the only way of learning new designs, as lacemakers had few other forms of instruction to help them.

Prickings made for lace to be produced commercially in long lengths had to be hard-wearing to withstand constant use. Parchment began to be replaced by card during the latter half of the last century. Today a good quality card is made specifically for pricking, and is available in several different thicknesses, the thinnest for the finest and closest-holed patterns. The pricking, apart from containing the pattern, also gives a degree of extra stability to the pins, thus contributing to the accuracy of the finished lace. If time and energy permit, it is best to use a pricking card, especially if the pattern is to be used many times over.

Today, for those who have not the time or the energy, the second-best option is the use of a photocopy. However, it is important to remember that photocopiers may not always copy to exactly the same size which, after repeated photocopying, could make quite a difference to a pattern.

It is intended that the patterns in this book should be photocopied, and that this method also be used for joining pattern sections together to make longer, complete pieces of lace. The photocopier can also be useful for enlarging some of the more complicated working diagrams for following, and for easier reading. The restricting size of the page has made it impossible to have the diagrams drawn any larger in this book.

When photocopying a pattern to work on, there are one or two possibilities to bear in mind. Working white threads on white paper, especially when the threads are fine, can be very difficult on the eyes. To avoid this problem, the photocopy can be made on thin tinted card (or paper, as long as there is some thin supporting card placed underneath this when working the pattern). If you make a photocopy on thin white card or paper, before working, cover this pattern with a layer of tinted, transparent, stick-on plastic film. For small patterns, in particular where the pinholes are marked by fine dots, choose only a lightly-tinted film such as pale grey, or pale turquoise-green. A blue film can be very difficult, and tends to obscure the fine dots when used under artificial lighting.

Separate photocopies of enlarged working diagrams can be a good idea, especially for anyone uncertain about the details of a new pattern. For easy reference, these separate copies can be coloured according to the colour coding system. Another idea for the beginner, or for someone trying a rather complicated pattern for the first time, is to place the photocopy of the working diagram on top of a styrofoam tile, (or something similar), so that as the pattern is worked, pins can be inserted into the corresponding pinholes on the working diagram. In this way there is a constant reminder of the point on the pattern that has been reached: this can be helpful if there is an interruption in the middle of working.

Pricking patterns
When pricking patterns, it is necessary to use a pin-vice, of which there are several different styles generally available, with wooden or metal handles. Choose one that is comfortable to hold. The best of these have four sections in the vice, which gives greater stability and grip to the needle being used. (If a pin is needed to prick with, just cut off the top ball end with a pair of pliers).

When the needle is in position in the pin-vice it should not extend more than 1 cm beyond the end, to reduce the likelihood of it breaking.

Never use a needle or a pin of larger diameter than the pin that is to be used to work with in the pattern. Too large a hole would allow the pins to move, causing distortion of the threads and therefore uneven work. For the same reason, it is necessary to prick the pattern at exactly the same angle as that at which the pins will be inserted.

Never make new prickings or patterns by pricking through from an already pricked card, as this can lead to inaccuracies, and badly distort the original pricking. If a new pattern from an existing pricking is required, and photocopying produces a copy too dark to work from, the best alternative is to use a photographic technique to make a contact print. In a darkened room, place the old pricking over a piece of photographically sensitive paper, and expose it briefly to the light. Remove the pricking and develop the paper as for other black and white photographic prints. If the original pricking was clear, this method produces an excellently clear, black and white pattern, which gets as close as possible to the original without damaging it. This print can then be traced, or photocopied and adjusted as necessary, and the pattern lines added to it. The result should be a good-quality new pattern. If photographic facilities are not available, local photographers will often make a copy cheaply.

Pricked patterns can take a good deal of time to make, but they will last a long time. It is therefore worthwhile doing the job well. A bad pattern and pricking will not make good lace!

The Belgian colour-coding system and the working diagram

The colour-coding system used extensively in Belgium today, along with the enlarged working diagram, was the brainchild of the School of Lace Teaching started in Brugge in 1911. This school was created specifically for the training of lace teachers. Their method of teaching, with the aid of large coloured diagrams, was so successful that it has now become the standard method of teaching lacemaking in Belgium today.

With more advanced patterns, where the movements of threads can become quite complex, a large working diagram becomes an invaluable aid as the colours indicate exactly what is required at any particular point on a pattern, without ambiguity.

In the working diagram, a single line indicates the movement of one pair of bobbins (unless it marked otherwise as a blue or yellow line). The dots mark the positions of the pins. To follow a diagram, simply follow the line of the pair of bobbins being worked and, on reaching the next pair of bobbins, work the stitch indicated by the colour of the intersection. Continue in this way, following the movement of the line of the pair of bobbins being worked.

The Belgian colour-coding system
RED   = Cloth stitch and twist
          (cross, twist, cross, twist)
          Whole stitch and twist
PURPLE = Cloth stitch (cross, twist,
          cross) Whole stitch
GREEN   = Half stitch (cross, twist)
YELLOW = The movement of an indi-
          vidual thread. This colour is
          frequently used to indicate
          the movement of a gimp
          thread
BLUE   = A two-pair plait
A short red line across another line indicates that that pair is twisted one extra

time; two short red lines indicate two extra twists to that pair, etc.

Colours for laces other than Flanders
ORANGE = Half stitch, pin, half stitch,
          twist (Dieppe ground –
          torchon variation)
BROWN = Half stitch, twist, pin, half
          stitch, twist (Torchon
          ground variation)
BLUE   = A two- or four-pair plait in
          Cluny Valencienne and
          Binche

The colour-coding in this book
Because of the limitations of colour printing, the number of colours in the working diagrams in this book have been reduced to four. For reference, the complete Belgian colouring system for working diagrams has been included above, and the only differences in this book are as follows:
---- = The movement of a gimp thread
=   = A two-pair plait
Also indicated:
J-----J = Join line position
C-----C = Corner turning point
S-----S = Suggested starting point
F-----F = Suggested finishing point
S   = Important that the securing
          technique should be used at
          this point

In the black-line working diagrams, where there is a particular technique that needs attention, the thicker black lines are equivalent to the red lines as in the coloured diagrams.

3

The Flanders ground

Historical note. The five-hole ground. Starting and finishing. The picot. Variations on the five-hole ground. Starting and finishing with a pattern. Joining two pieces of lace together.

Historical note

Towards the end of the sixteenth century plaited laces underwent a significant change, from a geometric to a floral and flowing style that used broader areas of cloth stitch in the form of tapes linked by plaits. These areas became so large and so frequent that the lace took on an oppressive, over-dense appearance. To compensate for this an edging pair was added to the tapes, thus opening out and defining the design more clearly, while at the same time lightening the general effect of the lace. This feature was retained, and remains a distinctive feature of the Belgian laces. The spaces between the areas of cloth stitch opened up, and with the need to carry pairs of threads from one cloth stitch area to another, two main methods developed. One continued to use the earlier method of plaits (which were frequently embellished with picots). It is from this style that the Binche laces developed. The other method, perhaps inspired by the method of working the edging pairs, developed into the first simple torchon-grounded bobbin lace. It is from this second method that all the other continuous laces developed (see diagram 1). The simple torchon ground was freely worked according to the requirements of the pattern, and without a grid. The result

was a rather irregular appearance. It is most likely that this torchon ground was the basis of the five-hole ground, and that it developed in the following way.

Until about 1620 the linen threads for lacemaking had been very heavy. As fashion demanded lighter laces to enhance clothing, it became necessary, with the introduction of the finer threads, to carry more in the ground but using the same amount of space. These extra threads were needed to cope with the increasingly complex floral patterns that were becoming fashionable. One solution to the problem was to use the same general torchon movement of threads in the ground, but doubling the number of pairs. The result was the five-hole ground (see diagram 5). Like the torchon, the five-hole ground was at first worked without a grid, but as the patterns increased in complexity and the spaces between the cloth stitch areas opened up, it became necessary to introduce a grid at an angle of 45° (V2H2).

The late seventeenth and eighteenth centuries were a time of great experimentation with grounds and fillings. The success of the five-hole ground was largely because of its stability and durability. For nearly 100 years the five-hole ground was made almost entirely in cloth stitch and twist, imitating its torchon parent. The next stage in its development was also a

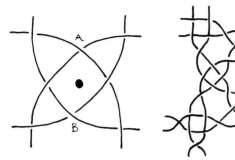 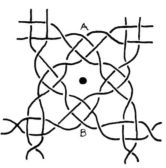 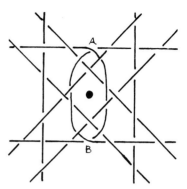

Fig. 1a. Original torchon

Fig. 1b. Five-hole ground worked entirely in cloth stitch and twist

Fig. 1c. Modern five-hole ground

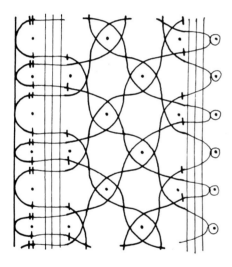 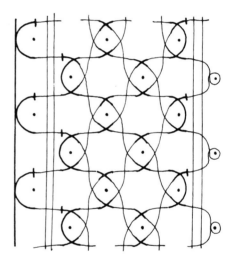

Fig. 2a. Old five-hole ground with edgings

Fig. 2b. Modern five-hole ground with edgings

DIAGRAM 5. *Stages in the development of the modern five-hole ground*

response to the requirements of fashion for a lighter and more delicate look to the ground, which resulted in the five-hole ground as more commonly used today. The cloth stitch and twist was retained at points A and B (see diagram 5) but all other points were worked in half stitch. The result was not only a lighter-looking ground, but also one that was quicker to make; time cost money!

21

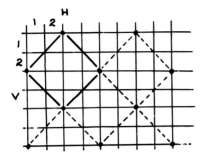

Fig. 1. Ground grid construction of V2 H2

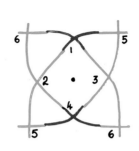

Fig. 2a. Working diagram of the five-hole ground with its working order

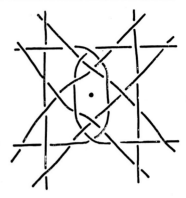

Fig. 2b. Individual thread movements of the five-hole ground

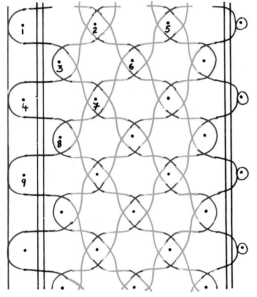

Fig. 3a. Ground working diagram with working order

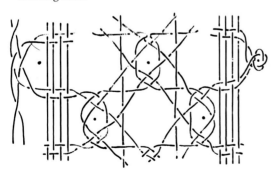

Fig. 3b. Individual thread movements for Fig. 3a

DIAGRAM 6.

The five-hole ground

The five-hole ground is worked on the same angled grid as that for the torchon ground. In Belgium the grid angle is described in terms of horizontal and vertical squares, and the angle is calculated on squared paper (see diagram 6 Fig 1). This method is straightforward to use and at the same time very accurate. The grid angle is drawn up in the following way. V stands for vertical, and H for horizontal. Diagonal lines are drawn from the opposite corners of the indicated squares, and in the case of the five-hole ground pinholes are marked at the points where the diagonals cross.

When making Flanders lace for the first time, it is essential to work a length of five-hole ground before attempting to work any of the patterns. After a little practice, the movements basic to the working of the ground should become second nature. Follow the numbered order of work for both the individual ground motif and the ground itself, as indicated by the numbers on diagram 6.

For a quick and accurate start, the five-hole ground pattern in diagram 6 can be photocopied. The numbers at the top of the working diagram of the ground indicate the number of pairs of bobbins required to start each section.

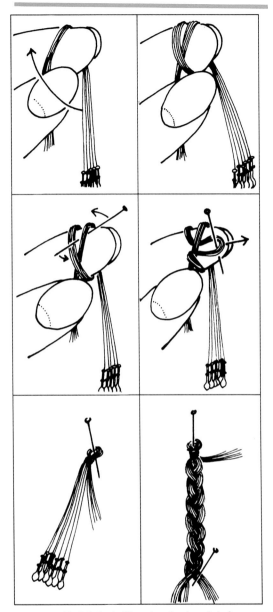

DIAGRAM 7. *Method of hanging the threads before starting the lace*

To start

For all the continuous Belgian laces, all bobbins are wound singly and then hung in groups on a pin about 3 cm above the intended starting position. The threads are then plaited very loosely level to the first pinhole (see diagram 7). This method of starting is very much quicker than winding the bobbins into pairs, and it makes no difference at all to the eventual join, because the pieces are overlapped, sewn together, and trimmed off neatly. (For the method of joining see p. 26) The only exceptions to this method are when starting certain special shapes, for example the brooch patterns in chapter 10, where the bobbins must be wound into pairs in order to start with a neat picot edge. Remember always to start the actual piece of lace at least 1-1½ cm before the intended join position, to allow for the overlap of the lace.

23

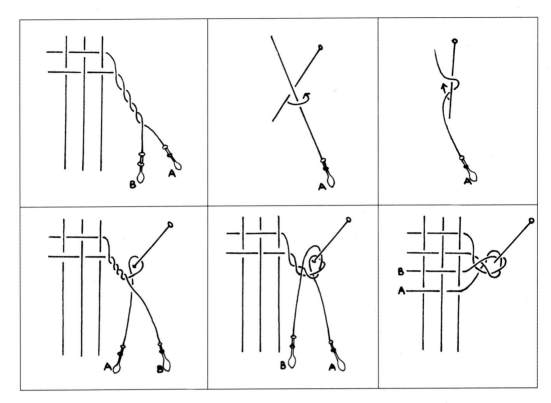

DIAGRAM 8. *Making a double picot*

The picot

The picots along the edge of Flanders lace are always double picots. The footside is always on the left in Belgian laces, and the picots always on the right (unless it is an insertion or special piece). To make perfect picots that do not come undone, pay great attention to the position of the threads.

After the position of the join line has been decided upon, it is necessary to start to work the pattern about 1-1½ cm before the intended position of the join. The larger the ground, the wider the piece of lace made before the join needs to be. When the lace has been almost completed and returned to the join line it is necessary to carry on working for a further 1-1½ cm (or more depending on ground size – but not for patterns in this book). In this way an overlap of an exactly matching pattern 2-3 cm wide is created.

To join the two pieces of lace together

The equipment required for this is one very short, very fine needle, a pair of finely-pointed scissors, and a joining thread that exactly matches the shade of the lace but is two counts finer.

Oversewing with the same size thread as the lace leaves a ridge, whereas completing the join with a finer thread reduces the size of the join ridge, making it far less noticeable and much neater.

To join the lace, place one end over the other so that the patterns match exactly. Pin the laces together in place on either side of the join line, with the pins going through the centres of the five-hole ground, as shown in the diagram, Fig. 2. Check at this point that the lace is not twisted before putting all the work into the sewing! Taking the needle and not too long a length of thread (if too long, a

| 1. Lace working diagram | 2. Ground motif with work order | 3. Individual thread movements | 4. Lace |

DIAGRAM 9. *Variations on the five-hole ground*

DIAGRAM 10.

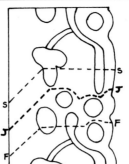

Fig. 1. Three different lace patterns showing possible starting, finishing and join positions

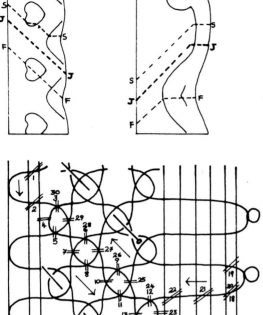

Fig. 2a. Order of work for joining lace

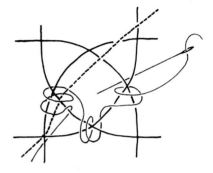

Fig. 2b. Method of sewing the ground to include the first running stitch (dotted line)

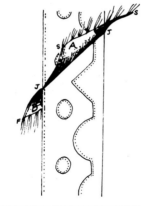

Fig. 3. Joined lace before trimming

length can easily become knotted and twisted), make a line of tiny running stitches through the centres of the five-hole ground following the join line. For the right-handed, this will be from right to left as they will be oversewing back along the tacking line from left to right. Do not make a knot in the end of the thread before starting; this would leave an unsightly lump in the lace. Start by oversewing a couple of running stitches. After reaching the footside with the running stitches, oversew the pairs back along the join line at the same time incorporating the running stitch following the order of sewing as shown in diagram 10 Fig. 2. The aim of the oversewing is to secure all the threads so that they cannot work loose or come undone.

When the join has been made, finish off the thread by running it back through the middle of the previous oversewing. With the sharp, finely-pointed scissors, trim away the spare lace as close to the oversewing as possible, taking great care not to cut the oversewing threads or the finished piece of lace (see flaps A and B in diagram 10 Fig. 3). The lace is now ready for mounting.

4

The pea motifs

Historical note. The pea motif and its variations. Introduction of the cloth stitch area. The gimp thread. Patterns.

Historical note

The pea motif is one of the earliest of the traditional shapes to be used within the ground. It first appeared in the Flemish laces in the first quarter of the seventeenth century. An example of this is shown in the photograph in diagram 11, taken from a piece of Antwerp lace. Working diagrams for this and two other early forms of pea accompany it. The pea motif in these early laces occurs only rarely, and then usually only in close connection with the floral part of the design. During the eighteenth century the pea motif was not used to decorate the five-hole ground at all, and only in the late nineteenth and twentieth centuries did the pea motif really find favour as a decoration to be added sparingly to the ground.

The first pea was somewhat square in shape, with an interesting technical feature frequently found at the beginning of cloth stitch areas in the older Flanders laces. This feature, shown in the working diagram, Figs. 2 and 3, as two black lines on either side of an intersection of threads (see A on the diagrams), is just a simple exchange of threads, but as a cross, not a complete half stitch. It is rarely used in twentieth-century Flanders lace, except in connection with snowball fillings.

Another distinctive feature of the area of cloth stitch in Belgian laces is the outlining pair. This is a pair of threads that follows the outer edge of the cloth stitch but is kept separate from it by the twists of the weavers of passives that enter and leave the area of cloth stitch. In the older laces this outlining pair was frequently separated from the cloth stitch by two twists, but in later laces and in twentieth-century Flanders lace it is separated by only one twist. Compare diagrams 11 and 13. See also p. 20, historical note on the background to the outlining pair.

The cloth stitch area has a distinctive and very typically Flemish technique for working the pairs that join and leave, a technique that can be traced back as far as the first Antwerp laces. This method of tension control and interchange of weavers, also found in Binche, Valencienne and Mechelen, could well have resulted from coping with the large number of threads entering and leaving the ground. It is a neater way of finishing off the cloth stitch area than retaining the same pair of weavers, and is shown in diagram 12.

In the old Flanders continuous laces a gimp thread was not consistently introduced until the first quarter of the eighteenth century, where it appeared in samples of Mechelen lace, and later, when it became a defining feature. Without the gimp, a smooth edge to the cloth stitch area was achieved by clever movement of pairs of threads. This method can be seen

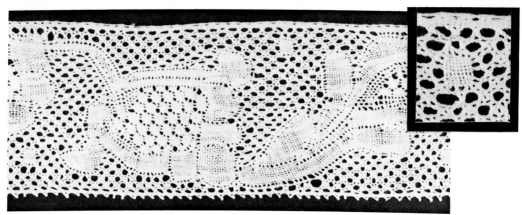

Fig. 1. 17th century Antwerp lace showing an early pea motif

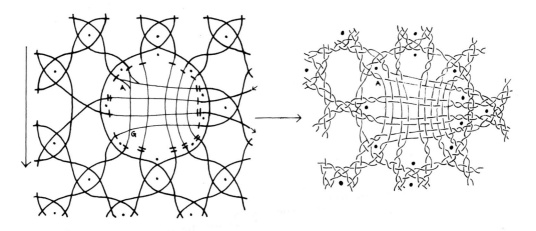

Fig. 2. Working diagram and individual thread movement diagram for the pea in Fig. 1.

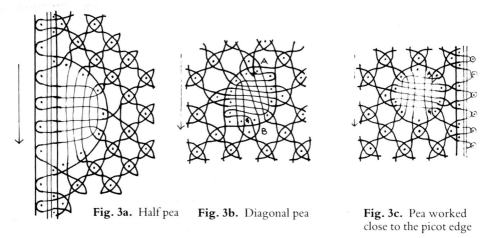

Fig. 3a. Half pea   **Fig. 3b.** Diagonal pea   **Fig. 3c.** Pea worked close to the picot edge

Fig. 3. Three other pea variations from old laces

DIAGRAM 11.

28

in some of the more advanced patterns in chapter 10. The skilled movement of threads helped to create a richness of movement in the design which can be lost somewhat when a gimp thread is used on its own.

A feature of life during the second half of the nineteenth century was its interest in the past. Lace did not escape these trends. Modern Flanders lace evolved as a reaction to the ever-changing commercial demands of the lace market, coupled with the desire to resurrect ideas from the past. The lace industry was in severe decline in the second half of the nineteenth century. Designers of bobbin lace were desperately looking for new ideas to compete against the ever-increasing adaptability of lacemaking machines. Against this background it is easy to see the roots of twentieth-century Flanders lace. It took the basic technique of the five-hole ground from the old Flanders laces, and the gimp outlining thread from the Mechelen. These elements were then combined with a simplification of fillings and techniques. A cotton thread, thicker than had been used in the eighteenth-century linen laces, resulted in a lace that was more speedily worked but somewhat heavier in both feel and design.

The pea and its variations

There are a number of variations on the basic pea shape, and some are shown in this chapter. The pea motif introduces the beginner in this lace to the technique of working a cloth stitch area into the Flanders ground, which is common to most of the continuous Belgian laces. There is a continuous exchange of weavers, and the tension of the threads has to be carefully controlled to avoid distortions of the cloth stitch area; otherwise holes will appear that were not intended in the pattern!

The order of work has been numbered so that it is possible to follow the chart in

Fig. 1. Method used in Flanders lace

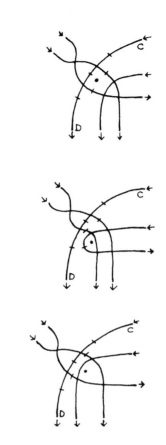

DIAGRAM 12. *Possible methods of introducing two pairs from the ground into the cloth stitch*

number order, and at each intersection of the threads the stitches are worked according to the colour of the lines on the diagram.

In diagram 13 at the beginning and end of the pea shapes at A and B (Figs. 1 and 2) there are two main methods for working pairs entering and leaving the area of cloth stitch. In both, two pairs of threads form the outlining pairs, while the other two enter the area of cloth stitch. In Fig. 1 only one pin is used for this technique; in Fig. 2, two pins are used. As can be seen from the diagrams, the resulting difference in shape is quite noticeable.

29

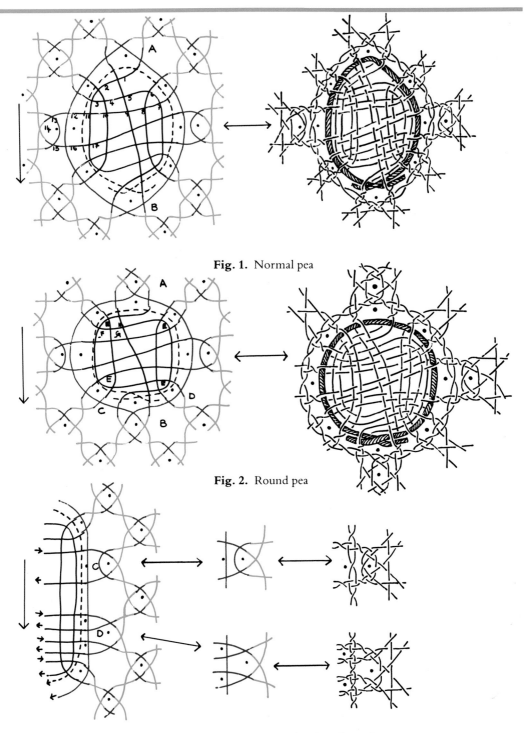

Fig. 1. Normal pea

Fig. 2. Round pea

Fig. 3. Two main methods of exchanging pairs at the side of the cloth stitch

DIAGRAM 13. *Pea motif*

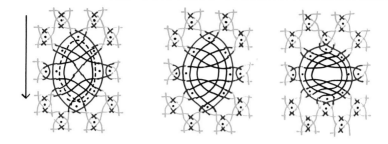

Fig. 1. Small peas with holes

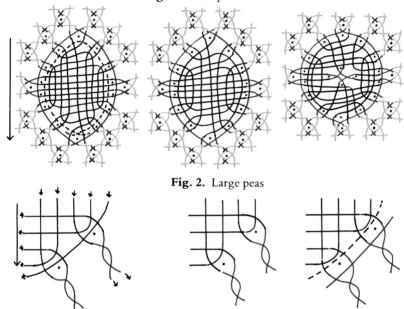

Fig. 2. Large peas

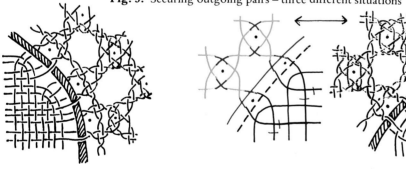

Fig. 3. Securing outgoing pairs – three different situations

Fig. 4. Securing incoming pairs – usual gimp technique

Fig. 5. Alternate methods of working the gimp thread to hold it more on the surface of the lace

DIAGRAM 14. *Pea variations*

Where the sides of a cloth stitch area run parallel with the footside and the picot edge, there are two basic methods by which the threads enter and leave the cloth stitch. These are illustrated in Fig. 3 at points C and D. Note the working direction of the threads and the difference in pinhole positions.

When working the cloth stitch area, care has to be taken with the tensioning of the threads, particularly at points marked E in Fig. 2, where there is an exchange of weavers. If, after completing the exchange of pairs, the pair marked with an F is pulled, the cloth stitch will move away from the outlining pair. To correct this, gently pull pairs G and H at the same time and the exchange of pairs will be pushed back into their correct position. Pulling gently with the weaver pair (H), after working it across to the other side of the cloth stitch, will also help to maintain good thread positions. A technique sometimes used to help secure these threads where the pairs enter the cloth stitch is shown in diagram 14 Fig. 5, where pairs G and H make an extra twist and cross.

Securing the positions of pairs leaving the cloth stitch is not always necessary but is occasionally essential. In these cases use a simple cloth stitch and twist twice with the leaving pair after they have passed through the outlining pair (Fig. 3c), or at certain points within a cloth stitch area (Figs 3a and 3b). These two cloth stitch and twists are always undone before recommencing working with the pairs concerned.

Diagram 14 shows some variations on the pea shape. The first three have holes added as a decorative feature. Any of these three methods can be used instead of the more usual peas to add interest to a pattern.

In the larger three pea shapes, the first has the conventional movement of pairs and gimp, while the second omits the gimp and compensates for this by a different movement of pairs. The third contains an 'oeil de perdrix' motif. Any three of these could be also substituted for the large pea motif in a pattern.

Gimp threads are always wound singly unless, as is the case in the pea motif, the pattern requires that the gimp be wound into pairs to start two sides of a shape from the same point. Single gimp threads are hung on a pin in the same way as the other pairs of bobbins at the start of a piece of lace. Any subsequent paired gimp thread additions are usually wound into pairs, and are hung temporarily on a pin at the edge of the pattern. The pin is removed and the threads pulled up as soon as there is enough cloth stitch area to support the gimp.

Gimp threads are worked singly with whichever thread happens to be on the outside of the cloth stitch area, and is not separated from this area by a twist as in some other laces (see diagram 13). The gimp threads are finished off by overlapping them at the appropriate point on the pattern, and they are caught in place by the tension of the surrounding threads, as shown in diagram 13 Figs 1 and 2.

An interesting variation on the working of the gimp thread is shown in diagram 14 Fig. 4, where the gimp is made to sit more on the surface of the lace by alternately working the gimp in with the cloth stitch and passing the next working pair underneath the gimp. The overall effect is a more strongly-defined outline to the pattern which can be very effective if used to offset a complicated filling. This technique also has the effect of creating a wrong and a right side to the lace.

Pattern I. 19 pairs
2 gimp (joined)

Pattern II. 23 pairs
1 gimp (single)
2 gimp (joined)

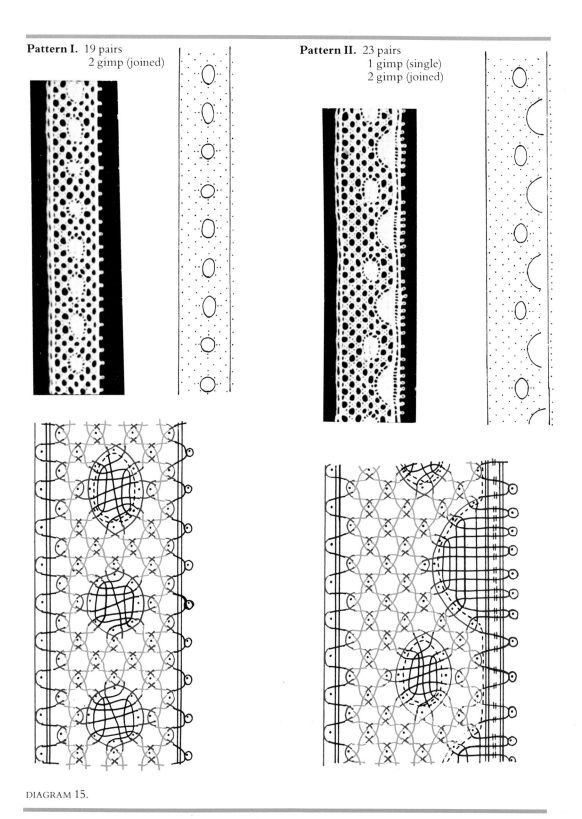

DIAGRAM 15.

Pattern III. 31 pairs

DIAGRAM 16.

34

Pattern IV. 25 pairs
2 gimp (joined)

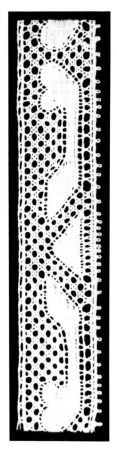
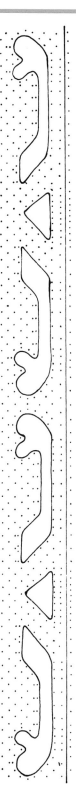
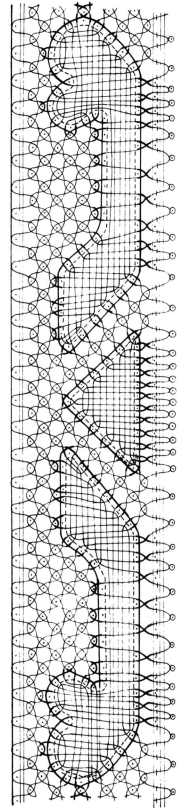

*This is an adaption of a frequently-found little clog
pattern. It is more commonly found as a single repeating
motif. There are many variations of this pattern*

DIAGRAM 17.

5

The corner

Historical note. Different techniques for working a corner. Methods of moving lace on a straight pillow, i.e. for corners and long lengths. Patterns.

Historical note

Before the mid-nineteenth century, most continuous bobbin lace was made commercially in straight lengths. If a piece of lace was required to fit around a corner, the lace was cut and re-joined at an angle, either gathered or pleated. Consequently, not many corners were designed specifically for working on the lace pillow. After the mid-nineteenth century, again as a result of commercial pressures, the bobbin lacemaking industry moved increasingly towards the more lucrative tourist market for which specially designed and shaped patterns were created to fit circular mats, special items of fashionable clothing and the like. The two World Wars severely affected Belgium and its economy, and the lace industry suffered so badly that it became almost non-existent. After the Second World War the lace industry revived, selling now to an increasing tourist trade in centres such as Brugges and Brussels. Visiting these places today, one will find many lace shops that include in their stock 'new' Flanders lace. Sadly there is only a very restricted range of patterns available to choose from, and the lace is made with rather coarse thread.

After the First World War, in many countries lacemaking became a craft for pleasure and interest. Some new and exciting work started to be created. Attractive, more modern pieces of lace were produced. Flanders lace was not excluded from this trend, and as manufacturing time was now no object and the commercial pressures had been lifted, some very time-consuming and large pieces were undertaken which included some very complicated and skilfully designed corners. Today, few people undertake such large works and more emphasis seems to be placed on using the Flanders lace tecniques in a freer, less constrained way than in pieces of continuous lace.

Corners

To work a corner in Flanders ground for the first time is not as difficult as it may appear initially. Remember to always work down to the turning point of the corner (marked on the relevant patterns in this book by a dotted line with a C at each end), and only then turn the lace 90° to the left to begin the next side. In this way one can avoid the problems of the apparent change of position of the cross twist sections of the ground (see diagram 18).

As with torchon, the angle of the grid makes a corner turn comparatively simple. The turning line neatly follows the angle of the ground. Diagram 18 shows the direction of working both before and after the corner (as indicated by the arrows). The position of the turning line can vary according to the pattern on the corner and the possible addition of pairs at the picot edge. Fig. 3 shows a variety of methods of turning a corner with some of the different possibilities of thread movements, for both picot and footside edges. Working diagrams accompany all the patterns in this book, and some of the different methods have been condensed here for reference and interest.

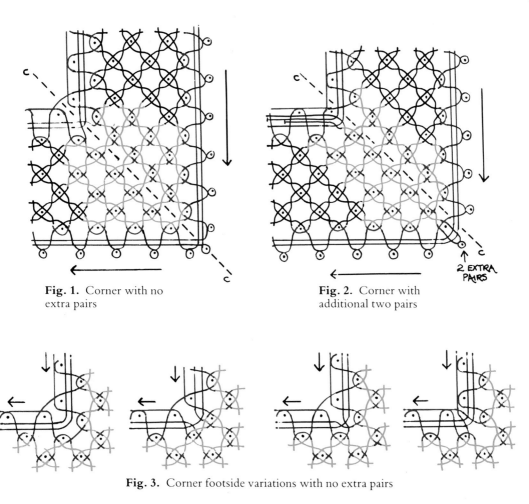

Fig. 1. Corner with no extra pairs

Fig. 2. Corner with additional two pairs

Fig. 3. Corner footside variations with no extra pairs

Fig. 4. Corner picot variations with no extra pairs

DIAGRAM 18. Methods of turning a corner

Motifs on a corner

While working a motif on a corner, it is essential to maintain a light tension on the threads to avoid enlarging any holes connected with the reduced number of pairs. To avoid this problem, a good pattern for the movements of the pairs should have been carefully worked out beforehand. In order to improve tension and at the same time increase the density of the cloth stitch area, pairs are often added. This addition and subtraction of a pair in a cloth stitch area is indicated in this book by a bar across the beginning and end of the pair involved. (See diagram 19 at points A and B.) To add in an extra pair, take two bobbins that have not been wound together into a pair, and hang them on a pin outside the pattern using the same technique that was used to start the lace (see diagram 7). The direction of the threads on entering the cloth stitch area should be such that there is no distortion of the cloth stitch. If the angle of entry is not correct, support the entry position of the threads by swinging them round an appropriately positioned pin that is already in the pattern. The extra pair is worked into the lace exactly as is shown in the diagrams, with no further pulling up. After the lace has been finished, these loose threads can be trimmed away. To remove a pair from the cloth stitch area, lift up the pair concerned, bringing the threads round a suitable pin in the pattern so that the threads in the cloth stitch area are kept in their correct position, and then pass the pair to the back of the lace, ensuring that the threads do not pull. This pair need not be cut off from the lace at this point, and it can be brought back into use if required. Loose threads can be carefully trimmed away later, after the lace has been removed from the pillow.

Note that in diagram 19 the method for the exchange of weavers (C) is the same as is used for the footside.

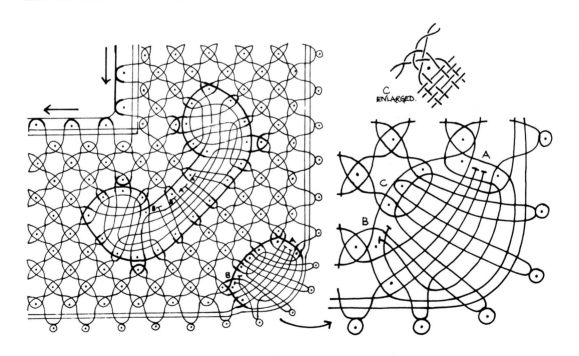

DIAGRAM 19. *Two motifs on a corner showing the adding and removal of extra cloth stitch pairs*

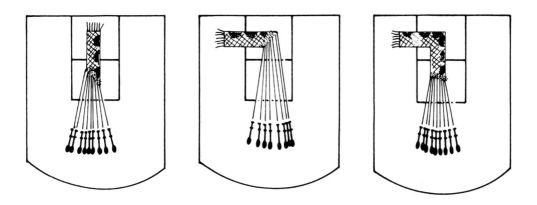

Fig. 1. Using a lace pillow with removable blocks

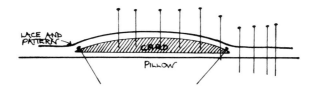

Fig. 2. Cross-section of lace and pattern on the lace pillow showing the pin positions and the extra card

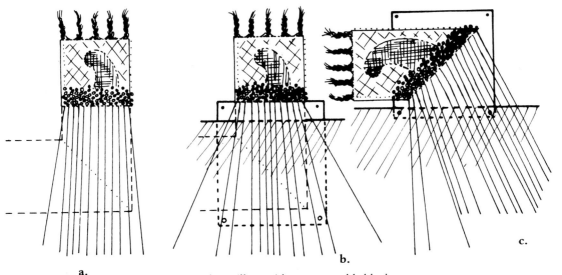

Fig. 3. A lace pillow without removable blocks, and showing the position of extra supporting card

DIAGRAM 20. *Methods of moving lace on a pillow*

To turn a corner

*Method 1, on a pillow with
removeable blocks*

When starting a piece of lace that has a corner and using a pillow with removeable blocks, it is important to think ahead. Plan the positioning of the pattern so that when one comes to work the corner, the pattern is correctly in the centre of the block (see diagram 20 Fig. 1) and the lace remains centrally positioned on the pillow.

*Method 2, on a pillow without
removeable blocks*

A piece of compacted polystyrene is required for this (e.g. from the flat tops of some egg-boxes); an alternative is the soft, thick card (also from egg-box tops). The size of the piece required depends entirely on the width of the lace and the size of the corner to be moved: it needs to be 2-3 cm wider than the edge of the pattern to allow easy handling. It is necessary to thin the card to a gradual slope on the two edges over which the lace will be worked. This avoids a lump or ridge that could show on the finished lace as a distortion of the pattern (see diagram 20 Figs 2 and 3).

Work down the piece of lace to within 2 cm of the opposite footside on the corner. Allow a larger distance if a coarse thread and large grid to the pattern is being used. Remove the cover cloth and then slide the piece of card underneath the threads and pattern, with the thinned edge as close to the pins at the bottom edge of the lace as possible. Secure the card in this position with a pin in each corner, and replace the cover cloth as in diagram 20 Fig. 3b. Continue to work up to the turning point at the position of the dotted line on the corner. If the lace is just being moved up the pillow, work down the lace until the other side of the cardboard is almost reached. It is important to ensure that the pins are inserted into the cardboard only, and do not penetrate the pillow itself; otherwise it will be very difficult to lift and move the cardboard. When there is a large number of bobbins, it is necessary to tie them carefully into bundles and lift them with the cover cloth before moving the lace, thus supporting their weight and preventing them from pulling and distorting the work. Remove the four corner pins from the cardboard, and any support pins from the pillow. Gently lift the cardboard with the lace away from the surface of the pillow until all the pins are free, and then – carefully supporting the weight of the bobbins at the same time – move the lace into its new position. As far as possible, gently ease any pinpoints back into the surface of the pillow and secure the card once again with a pin in each corner. Replace the cover cloth and pin into position (see Fig. 3c), undo the bundles of bobbins, replace the support pins, and all is ready to recommence. Note that this method is very useful for moving a piece of lace from one pillow to another; when doing this, however few bobbins you have, remember to always tie the bobbins together first and support their weight carefully while they are in transit.

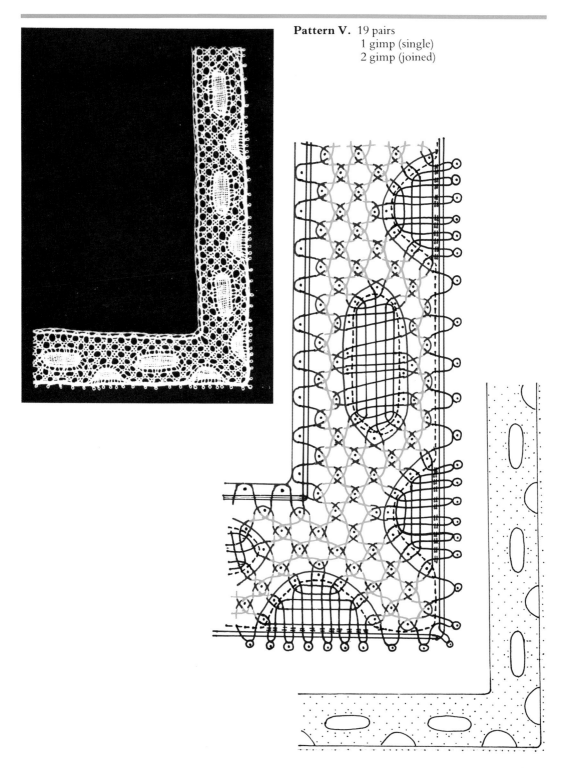

Pattern V. 19 pairs
1 gimp (single)
2 gimp (joined)

DIAGRAM 21.

Pattern VI. 26 Pairs
4 gimp (joined in pairs)

DIAGRAM 22.

6

Chevrons and wavy edges

Historical note. Methods of making chevrons. Patterns. Deep and shallow wavy edges to the lace on both the footside and the picot edge. Patterns.

Historical note

Scalloped picoted edges were in fashion at the very earliest moments of the evolution of the old Flanders lace. Techniques for coping with this shape have therefore been in use for a very long time. By the 1630s the fashion was for straight-edged laces, but during the eighteenth century gently curved and wavy edges came into fashion again.

Because of the large number of threads being carried in both the ground and cloth stitch areas, it is extremely difficult, without actually removing pairs from the lace, to make really deep curves. The edgings in the eighteenth-century laces used a chevron between the scallops to help create the illusion of an edge more deeply waved than was actually the case. The effect of the curve following the outline of the ornate flowery design was emphasised by an outlining gap, created by two twists of the weavers before and after entering the edging pairs. (This technique is used in the cat pattern, diagram 64.) In these eighteenth-century laces, the chevrons are almost always set into areas of cloth stitch, whereas in twentieth-century patterns chevrons can be found as design features in their own right surrounded by ground.

These older techniques of making chevrons were sometimes quite different from those in general use today, and are worth mentioning here. Many of the pieces of continuous lace made during the eighteenth century were intentionally designed with only half the pattern, so that two pieces of identically patterned lace could be joined carefully down the middle along a narrower footside, and be made into a cheaper form of lappet. The gently curved and dented picoted edge gave a little extra delicacy to the finished article, particularly when the lace was slightly gathered.

The present-day method of making chevrons

Although Flanders lace is traditionally a comparatively straight-edged lace, rounded edges occasionally occur in a design, and this usually means that there is a need for a chevron technique to link the curves together. It must be remembered that the chevrons shown here are just a few examples demonstrating the basic principles involved, and that there are many variations according to the needs of different patterns. When working a chevron, care must be taken to note the positions of the twists, particularly with reference to the central pair marked with an **A** on the diagrams, because they work differently in each example. The two basic techniques of making chevrons are illustrated in diagram 23. The older technique shown in Fig. 1 is now rarely used. Fig. 2 is also from an eighteenth-century lace and shows a chevron commonly used today when needed within an area of cloth stitch. The other chevrons in the diagram show a small selection of more modern chevrons set within the five-hole ground.

The wavy edge

The depth of curved edge possible within the limitations of the large numbers of threads on Flanders lace is controlled by the type of relay of weavers to picot or footside used (see diagram 28 points **A** and **B**).

The picot edge
Here it is necessary to maintain along the edge an even spreading of picots which hold the outside passives well, but do not overcrowd them. Allowing too much space in between the picots results in a very weak edge to the lace. The type of relay is chosen by the designer according to the number of picots required.

The footside
The guiding principles here are very much the same remembering that the footside usually has more weavers going out to the edge than would be the case for the picot edge. Patterns with a wavy footside are uncommon in Flanders lace but, when produced, the extra trouble involved in their mounting when made into handkerchiefs, mats, collars etc. is usually well worth the effort and care. The methods of working these edges will vary from pattern to pattern, but the basic principles will remain the same, as shown in diagram 28.

Figs. 1. and 2. 18th-century methods of making chevrons within a cloth stitch area

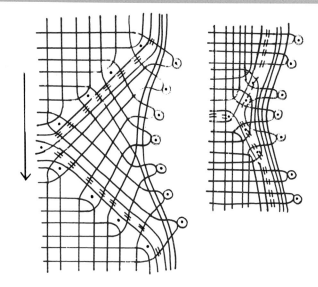

Figs. 3.-6. Chevrons within the ground

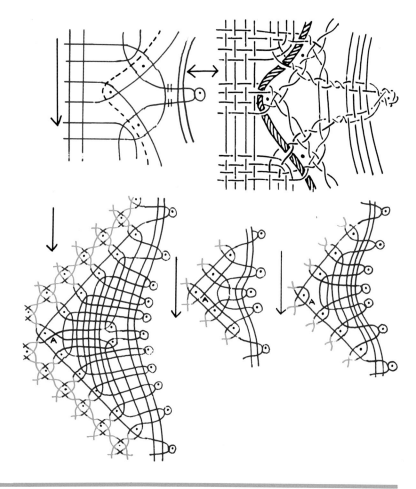

DIAGRAM 23. *Chevrons.*

Pattern VII. 24 pairs
1 gimp (single)
2 gimp (joined) – omit
if alternate non–gimp
heart shape method is
used.

In this pattern there are two optional methods of working the heart shape. The method using the gimp is shown in the lace sample

DIAGRAM 24.

46

Pattern VIII. 23 pairs

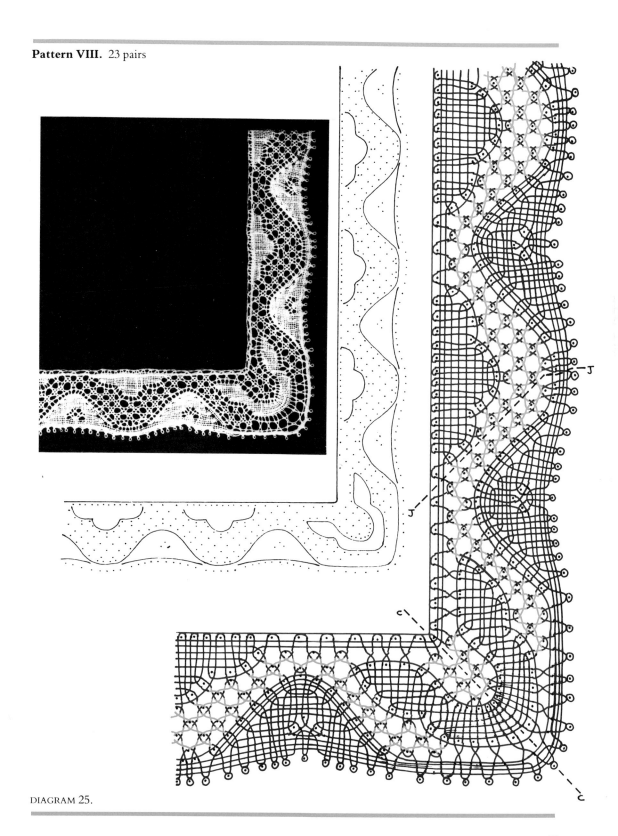

DIAGRAM 25.

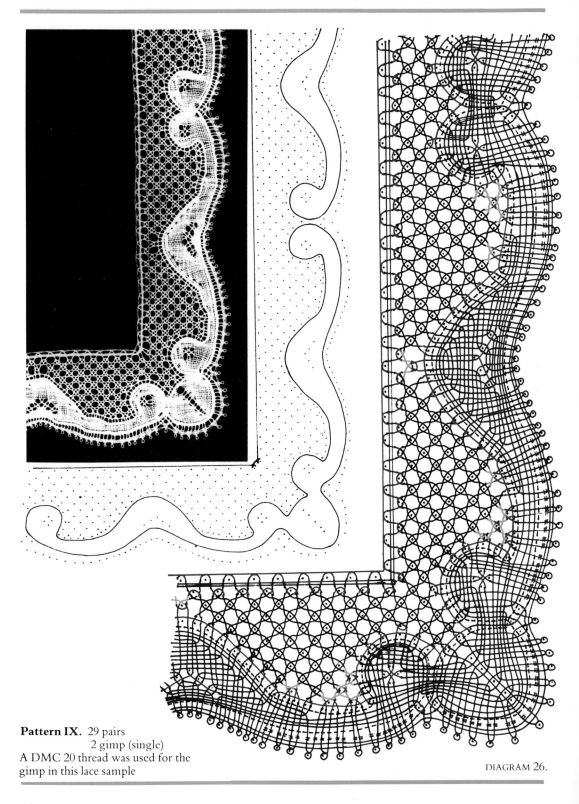

Pattern IX. 29 pairs
          2 gimp (single)
A DMC 20 thread was used for the
gimp in this lace sample

DIAGRAM 26.

48

Pattern X. 38 pairs, and five extra,
plus two for the corner

DIAGRAM 27.

DIAGRAM 27. (*continued*)

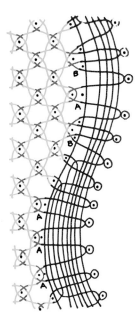

Fig. 1a Picot edge and shallow curve

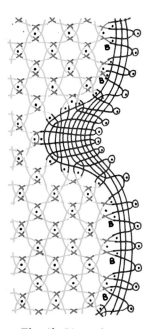

Fig. 1b Picot edge with deep curve

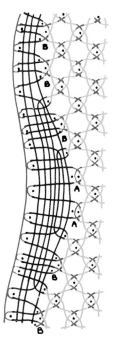

Fig. 2a Footside and shallow curve

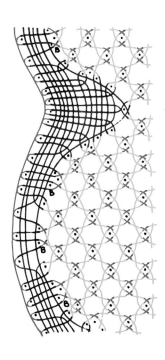

Fig. 2b Footside and deep curve

DIAGRAM 28. *Wavy edges*

51

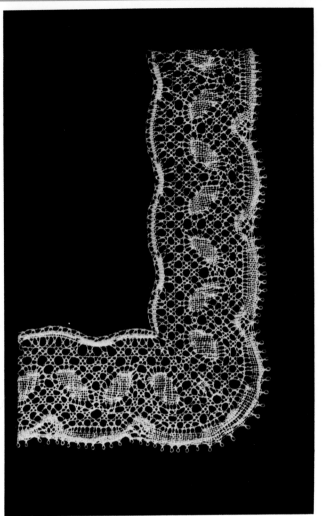

Pattern XI 32 pairs, plus one pair extra for the corner
Gimp threads could be used to enhance the edge and the oval shapes, if so add:
1 gimp (single)
2 gimp (joined)

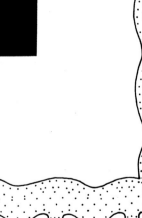

DIAGRAM 29.

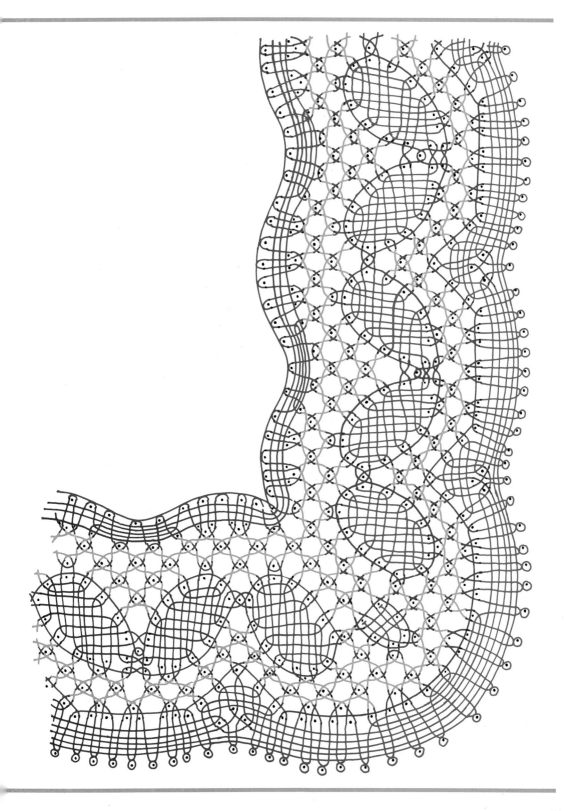

7

Holes and straight-line beginning and finishing of cloth stitch areas

Historical note. A selection of hole techniques. Methods of dealing with the ground between cloth stitch areas. Half stitch areas within the cloth stitch. Variations on the Monkey pattern. The straight line beginning and finishing of cloth stitch areas.

Historical note

There is a very large number of different methods for making intentional holes within an area of cloth stitch. The majority of these have been in use for a long time. The simplest, and possibly oldest, technique is the method of making a hole by just twisting the weavers or passives as in diagram 30 Fig. 1. This technique was primarily used for making linear holes in the cloth stitch which gave it lightness, life, form and movement. One distinctive fancy hole, shown in Fig. 4, can be seen in a large number of old laces, but less commonly seen is its half-stitch variation, which can look very pretty (see Fig. 4a). There are variations on this type of hole depending on the number and position of the twists.

Holes

A variety of hole techniques have been included in this chapter for two reasons. The first is that these pages may act as a useful reference point for techniques. Second, more experimentally-minded lacemakers may like to add a little extra detail and interest to their existing or new patterns. All the diagrams indicate the working direction of the threads where necessary, and are positioned in their correct working direction. When adding

one of these techniques to an existing area of cloth stitch it is necessary to place the hole carefully in a position that will maintain the appropriate thread movement. It may be necessary to rearrange the thread sequence according to the requirements of the hole to be included.

Special techniques for the movement of pairs between areas of cloth stitch
To help practise most of the more commonly-used techniques of moving between the cloth stitch and footside, and cloth stitch and picot edging areas of the lace, as many as possible have been condensed into the first monkey pattern (diagram 33). Enlargements of some of these methods plus one or two similar variations are shown in diagram 31. The positions of the pinholes in relation to the threads vary slightly from one broadly similar example to another.

The area of half stitch within a cloth stitch area
In some patterns an area of half stitch is worked within the cloth stitch in order to create extra interest and contrast. The Monkey pattern, of which many variations are commonly found in modern Flanders lace, is a good example, as it has a half stitch area forming part of the 'head' as a very distinctive design feature.

The half stitch area can usually be

identified on a pattern by its surrounding line of pinholes, meant to support the threads as they change direction from cloth stitch to half stitch and vice-versa, leaving a neater finish. Not all half stitch areas have supporting pins, particularly small ones. See diagram 32 for details of working this cloth stitch containing a half stitch area (where the latter area is indicated by green, and the cloth stitch by purple).

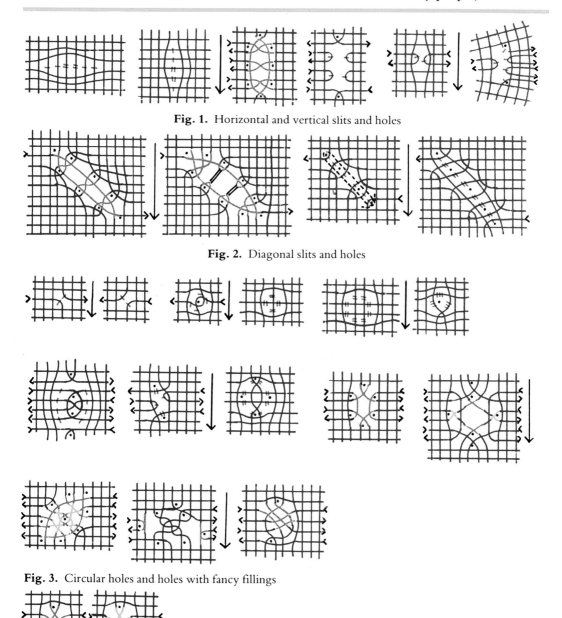

Fig. 1. Horizontal and vertical slits and holes

Fig. 2. Diagonal slits and holes

Fig. 3. Circular holes and holes with fancy fillings

Fig. 4. '*l'oeil de perdrix*'

DIAGRAM 30.

55

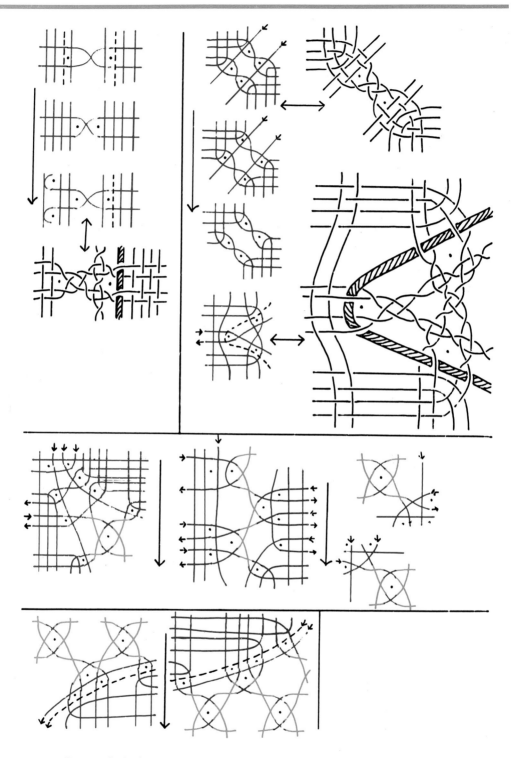

DIAGRAM 31. *Different methods of moving pairs between areas of cloth stitch and their variations*

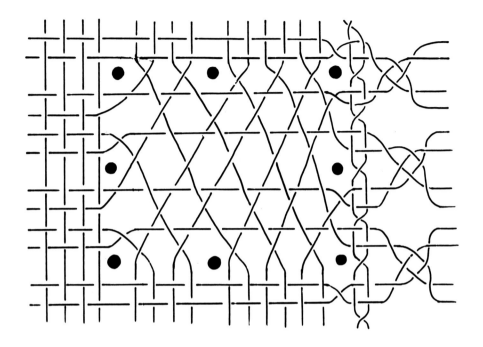

Fig. 1. Individual thread movements

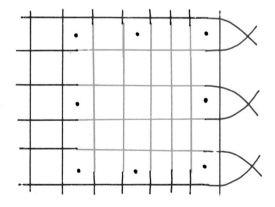

Fig. 2. Working diagram for Fig. 1

DIAGRAM 32. Enclosed half stitch area

57

Pattern XII. 29 pairs

This monkey pattern includes most of the most commonly-found techniques used in Flanders lace excepting the gimp.

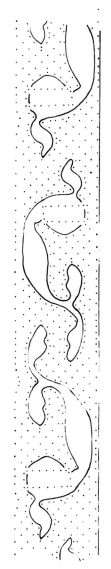

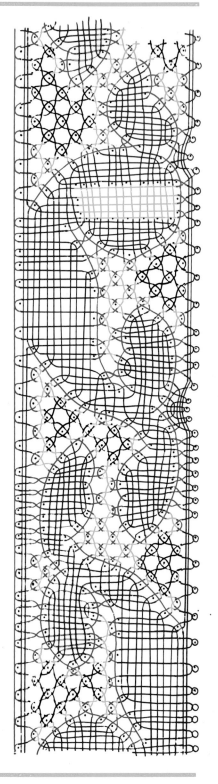

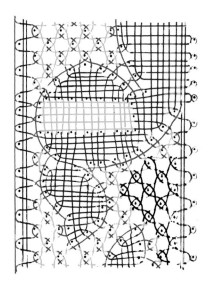

DIAGRAM 33.

Fig. 1. Pattern XIII

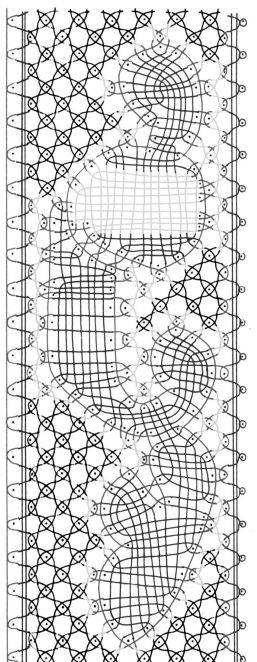

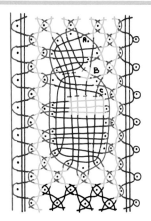

Fig. 2. Pattern XIV (Baby monkey)

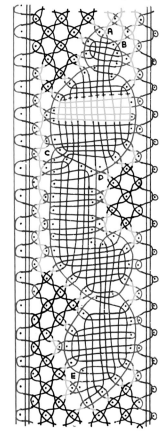

Fig. 3. Pattern XV

DIAGRAM 34. *Three monkey patterns. There are many variations on the monkey. Some older patterns include simple flowers, more recent patterns are usually very basic.* **Fig. 1** *has pretty movements of threads,* **Fig. 2** *is a good basic monkey pattern, and* **Fig. 3** *is a lovely little monkey pattern which has some interesting thread movements*

Fig. 1. Pattern XIII. 31 pairs **Fig. 2. Pattern XIV** 21 pairs **Fig. 3. Pattern XV** 23 pairs

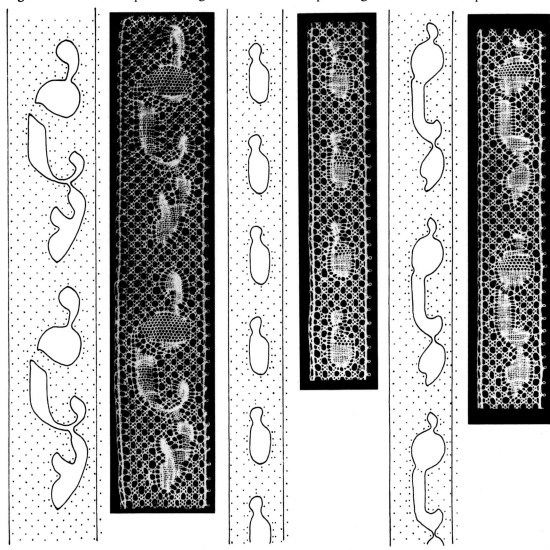

DIAGRAM 35.

60

Straight-line beginning and finishing of an area of cloth stitch

The straight-line beginning and finishing of a cloth stitch area on a line at right angles to the footside requires some special techniques. There are two methods, shown in diagram 36. Fig. 1 shows the method using a continuous outlining pair, and Fig. 2 shows a method whereby an effect of an outlining pair is created by the crossing of pairs of passives in cloth stitch and twist (shown on the working diagram in red).

Fig. 1. With an outlining pair

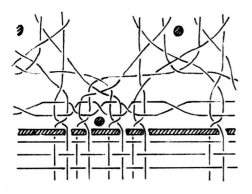

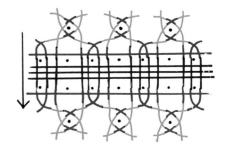

Fig. 2. Illusion of an outlining pair

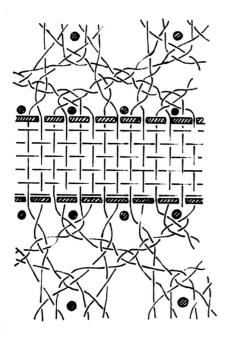

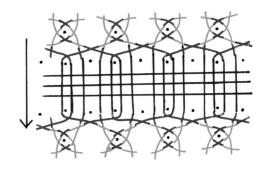

DIAGRAM 36. *Straight line beginning and finishing of cloth stitch areas*

Pattern XVI. 32 pairs, plus two
extra for the corner

DIAGRAM 37.

Pattern XVII. 33 pairs, plus one
extra for the corner

DIAGRAM 38.

8

The double-pointed corner

The feature of the corner, as mentioned in chapter 5, is a late nineteenth and early twentieth-century introduction. It can be an interesting challenge to the designer faced with the problems of moving the threads in a cloth stitch area to turn them smoothly through 90°. If two of these right-angled corners are placed next to each other, they form between them another 90° angle that turns in the opposite direction (see diagram 39 Fig. 1). This simple doubling-up of a corner has many possibilities. If the method of doubling-up the corners is repeated several times over along the length of a piece of lace, a very different-looking Flanders lace results. One achieves not only a sharply-pointed or rounded edge which is impossible to achieve in any other more conventional way, but also a strikingly different look to the basic five-hole ground. Diagram 39 Figs. 2 and 3 show some possibilities for varying the corners.

Diagram 40 Fig. 1 shows how this cornering technique can be taken a stage further to create shapes that need to be joined together, whether in part or completely.

The joining of this lace can be done after it has been removed from the lace pillow by carefully sewing the footsides together, or it can be joined whilst the lace is still being worked on the pillow by a hooking-in technique (the same method as is used in the non-continuous laces such as Duchesse, Rosaline, or Honiton). This hooking-in technique is not traditionally associated with Flanders lace. Diagram 40 Fig. 2 shows the basic working diagram for making such a shape that requires this latter method of joining. Fig. 3 shows a more detailed diagram of the process of hooking-in, which can be done with any of the traditionally-used pieces of equipment made for this purpose, such as a small crochet hook, bent needlepin, etc. Do not use a wig hook as this can tear and weaken the threads.

Method of hooking-in
Do not remove the pin from the loop which is to be hooked into unless this is absolutely necessary. Insert the end of the crochet hook (needle pin) into the appropriate loop of the previously worked looped edge, marked A in the diagram. Pull thread B through the loop. Pass the other thread C bobbin-end first through the loop which has just been made with thread B, gently pull the threads down by the bobbins, and then slide out the hook. Carefully ease the threads into their final positions and twist once.

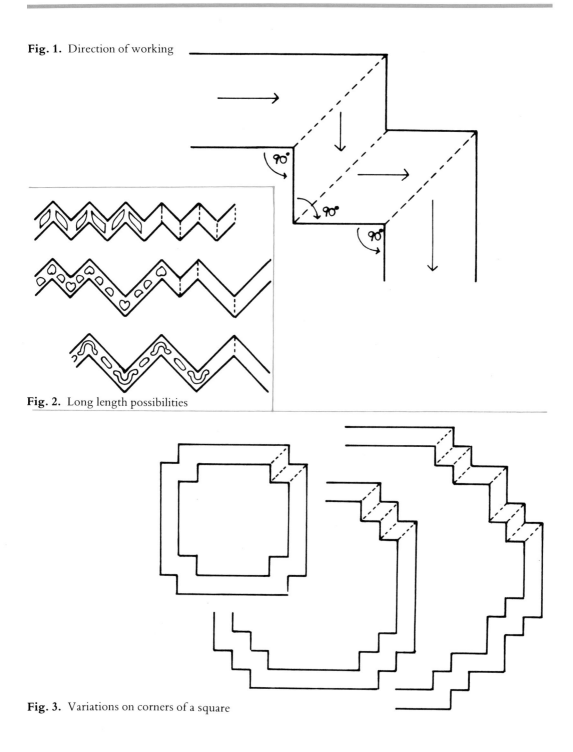

Fig. 1. Direction of working

Fig. 2. Long length possibilities

Fig. 3. Variations on corners of a square

DIAGRAM 39. *The double-pointed corner*

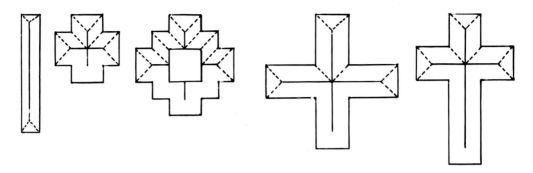

Fig. 1. Shape possibilities

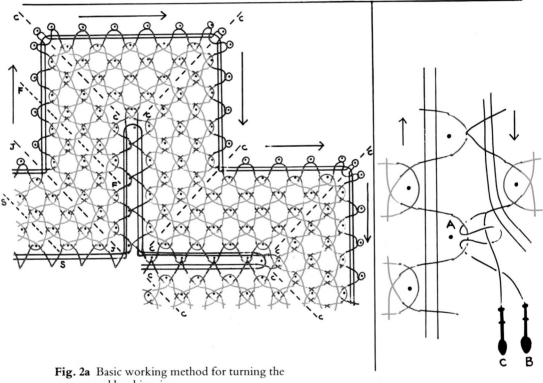

Fig. 2a Basic working method for turning the corners and hooking-in

Fig. 2b Hooking-in detail

DIAGRAM 40. *The joined-up double-pointed corner*

Pattern XVIII 23 pairs
2 gimp (joined)

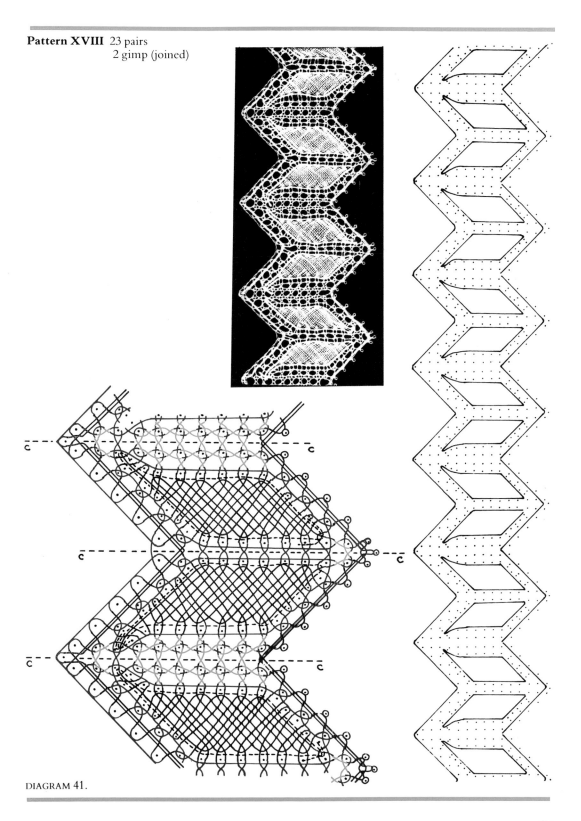

DIAGRAM 41.

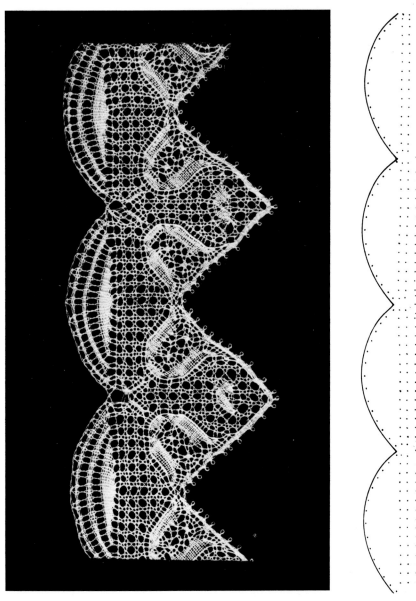
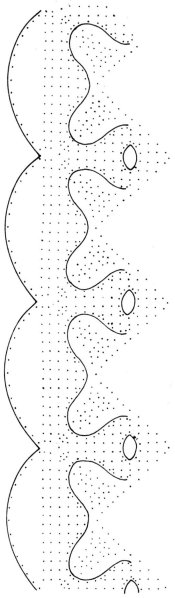

DIAGRAM 42.

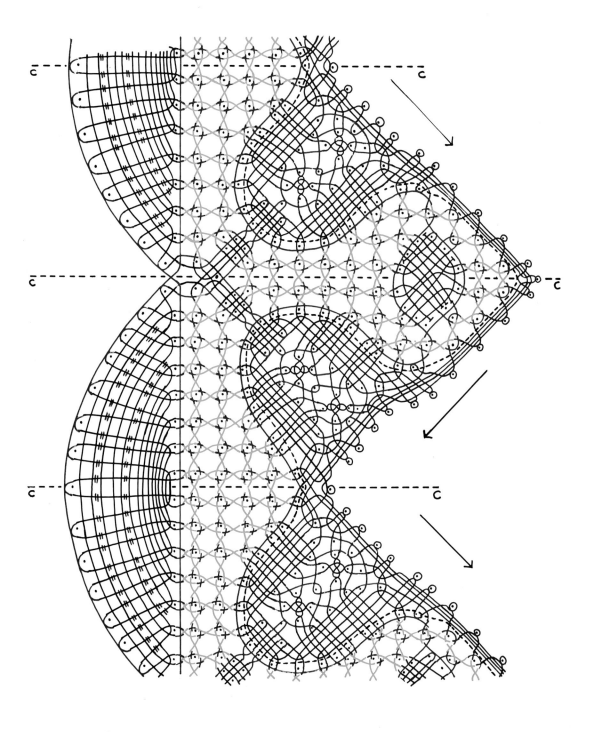

DIAGRAM 43. *Working diagram for pattern* **XIX**

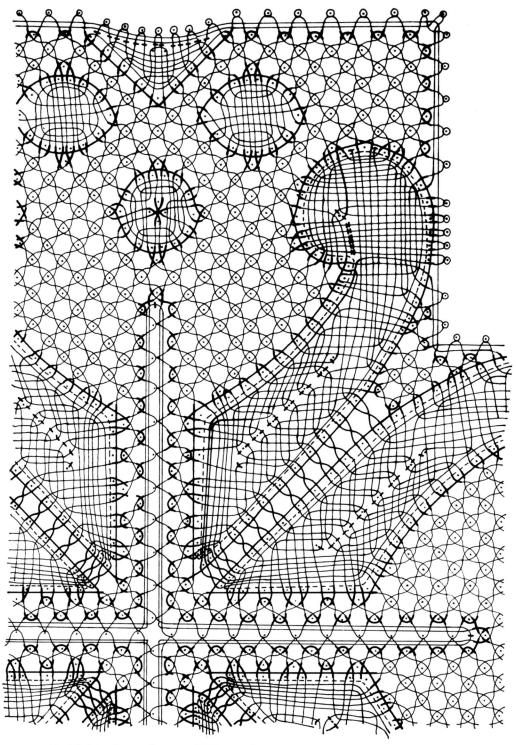

DIAGRAM 44. *Working diagram for pattern* **XX**

Pattern XX 38 pairs plus two for
the motif. 2 gimp (joined)
*Gimp threads could be used to good effect
in this pattern, in particular the raised
gimp technique for the main cloth stitch
area (see diagram 14. Fig. 4). It is
intended that the centre of this pattern
should be hooked-in*

DIAGRAM 45.

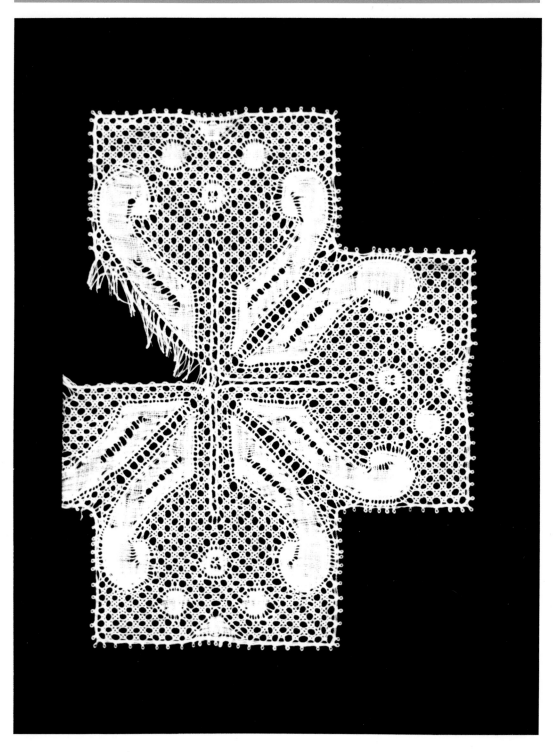

DIAGRAM 45. (*continued*)

9

Fillings

Historical note. Snowflakes and their variations. Snowballs and their variations. Patterns.

Historical note

Fillings developed with the demand for more detail, decoration, and delicacy within lace designs; a wide variety of fillings were in frequent use in the early piece laces, and some of these were adapted to the continuous laces. For example simple snowballs, together with the fillings shown in diagram 57, were in general use during the first quarter of the seventeenth century. The development of these design features was rapid, and by the beginning of the eighteenth century, a number of variations were in general use. the next hundred years saw fillings attain amazing levels of complexity and fineness. The types of filling connected with the laces with a five-hole ground can, with only a few exceptions, be placed in two main categories based on their thread movement and grids. One is the snowflake, the other is the snowball.

The snowflake fillings are divided into two main groups, the large and the small. In both of these, the pairs from opposite sides cross each other in the centre in a very characteristic movement.

The snowball filling pairs move round each other creating a round, usually dense, area of cloth stitch.

During the first quarter of the twentieth century, the increasing pressures of commercialism, coupled with the decline in design skills, the demand for simple laces that were quick to make, and the accompanying reduction in the number of pairs used in a pattern, all resulted in a

| **Fig. 1.** Snowball | **Fig. 2.** Large snowflake | **Fig. 3.** Small snowflake |

 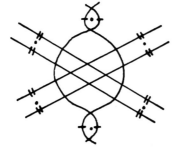 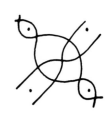

DIAGRAM 46. *Basic filling shapes*

greatly reduced selection of fillings being in general use. The majority of patterns used only a limited number of snowflake variations.

General note

It will be noticed that all fillings in Flanders lace are surrounded by an area of cloth stitch. This is because fillings are worked on a different-angled grid to that of the ground (V2 H2), and the cloth stitch area accommodates this change of direction. It also allows only the required number of pairs to move into the filling, retaining the extra pairs within the area of cloth stitch, which also provides a visual barrier between one busy part of the lace design and another, so that the resulting lace is pleasing to the eye. To successfully produce a good filling, it is also very important to have the right ratio of thread to the size of the grid; otherwise, if the threads are too fine or the grid too large in relation to the cloth stitch area, the threads will not be close enough to show up the shapes they are supposed to form when worked together and the beauty of the filling could be lost. Too thick a thread, or too small a grid, would have the opposite effect and give too dense a look.

Concerning the making of fillings, the other very important point to notice is the position of the pinholes. If these are not placed in the correct position, the tensions and spacing of the threads will be wrong, and the end result may not look as it should. In some cases incorrect pin positions can make a lace look very different from what was intended.

The final important feature of fillings is that there is usually no outlining pair separating the area of cloth stitch from the filling. Occasionally this is not the case: the pattern in diagram 52 is such an exception.

The large and small snowflake fillings have their own grids which do not vary. These fillings have been specially arranged so that any which use the same grid and same number of pairs can be exchanged and put into any pattern with those same conditions, thus giving more freedom and flexibility within an existing pattern.

On the right-hand side of each working diagram the way the ground liaises with the cloth stitch is shown.

The small snowflake

All the small snowflake fillings are worked on the same-angled grid, V1 H1 (90°), and they each have four pairs to work the motif, thus enabling any of the fillings to be substituted for any other in any pattern with a small snowflake grid.

The large snowflake

As for the small snowflake, all fillings are worked on the same-angled grid V1 H2 (26°), carrying six pairs, and are therefore interchangeable.

The snowball

Included in this section are a very small selection of fillings. As a result of limiting the number of pairs involved, the grid angles vary from filling to filling. There is no definite rule about this, but the nearer the shape of the grid to a 90° angle, the rounder will the resulting snowballs be.

If substituting a new filling into an existing pattern, ensure that the same number of pairs of threads are involved. In the older laces sometimes the snowballs were separated by a single row of threads, sometimes by many pairs in cloth or half stitch which gave the effect of a ball nestling between bars. In Mechelen lace these fillings became very involved, using large numbers of pairs.

Diagram 55 shows some snowball fillings without holes, and diagram 56 shows them with holes.

All fillings, particularly those that have central holes, require care with the tension control of the threads that might require some practice. It is for this reason that diagram 57 has been included, to practise the small and large snowflake fillings and their variations.

Fig. 1. Pattern grid VI HI

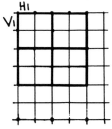

Fig. 2. Variations on the small snowflake pattern

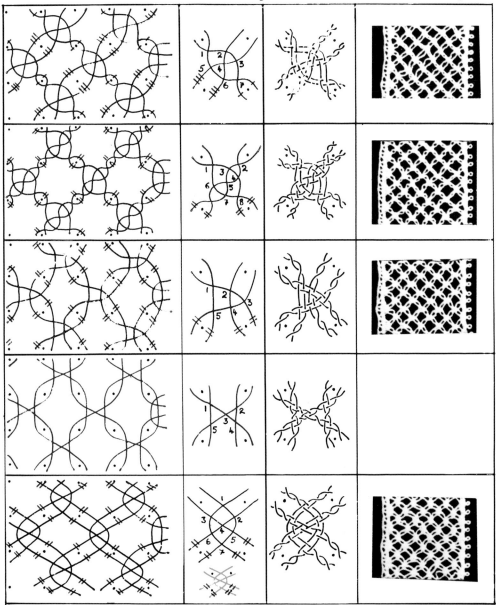

DIAGRAM 47. *The small snowflake fillings*

Fig. 1. The grid VI H2

Fig. 2. Variations

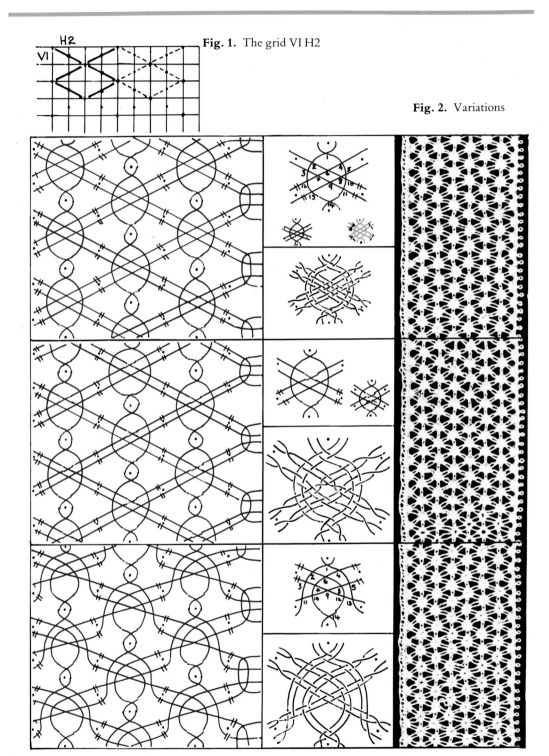

DIAGRAM 48. *The large snowflake and its variations*

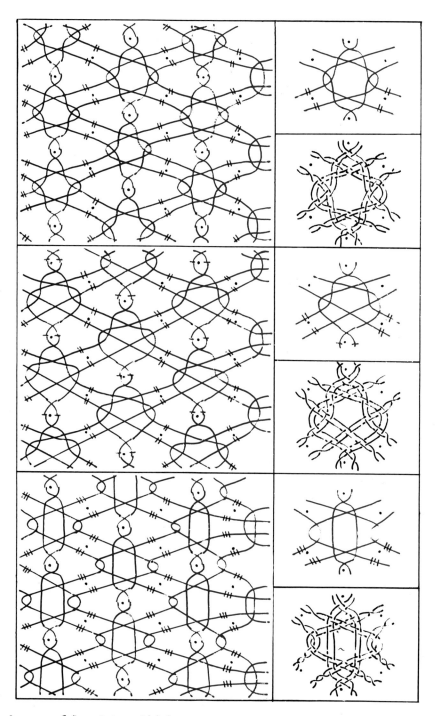

DIAGRAM 49. *Large snowflake variations with holes*

Fig. 1. Small snowflake

Fig. 2. Large snowflake (*This size grid works best with an Egyptian 70/2 thread*)

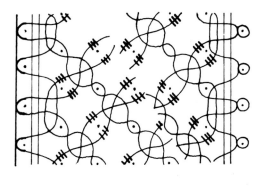

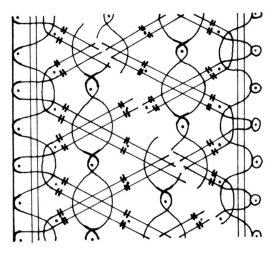

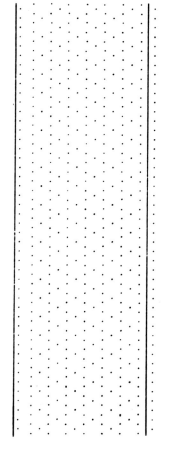

DIAGRAM 50.

Pattern XXI 25 pairs
4 gimp (joined in pairs)

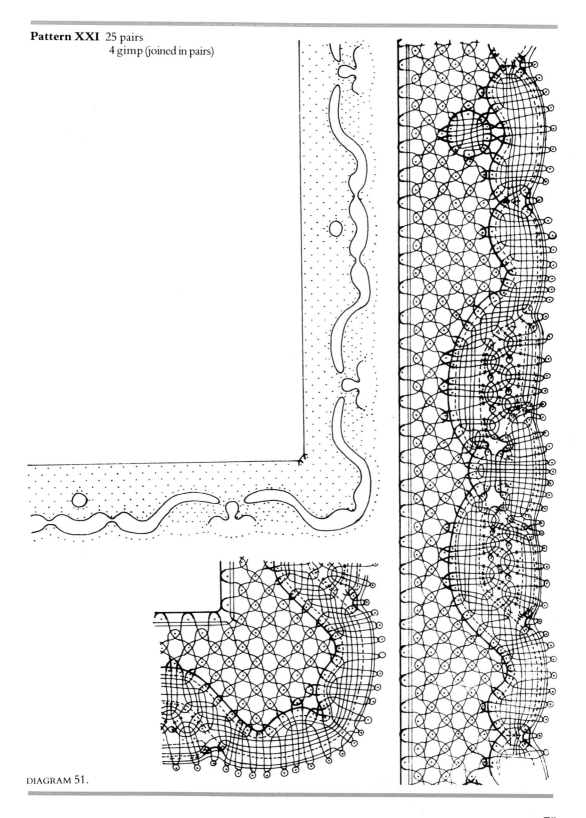

DIAGRAM 51.

79

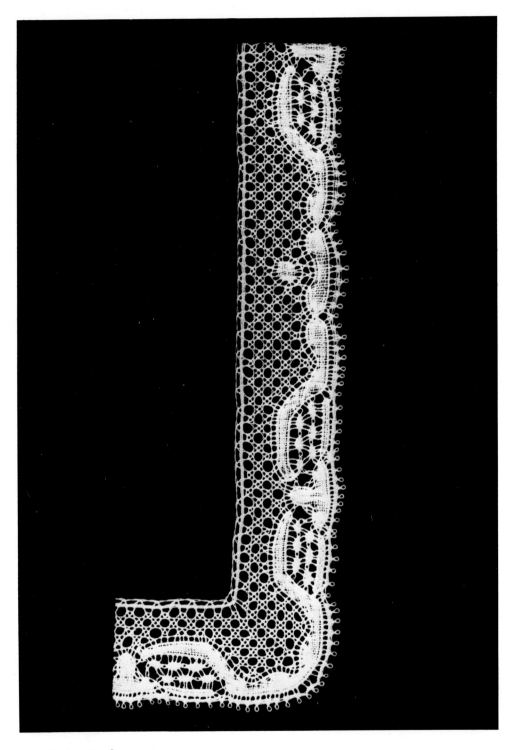

DIAGRAM 51. (*continued*)

Pattern XXII

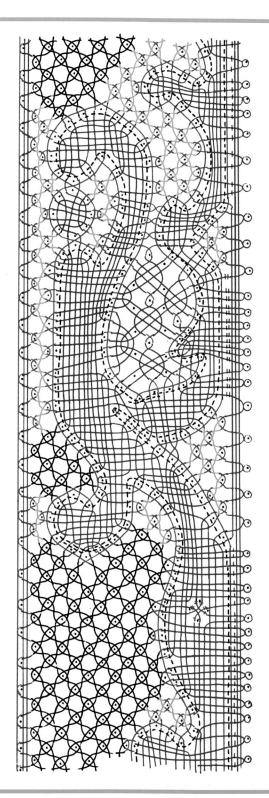

DIAGRAM 52.

Pattern XXII 37 pairs
          2 gimp (single)
          2 gimp (joined)
This pattern contains the more unusual feature of an outlining pair separating the cloth stitch from the filling areas. This pattern is based on a motif from a pattern made earlier this century

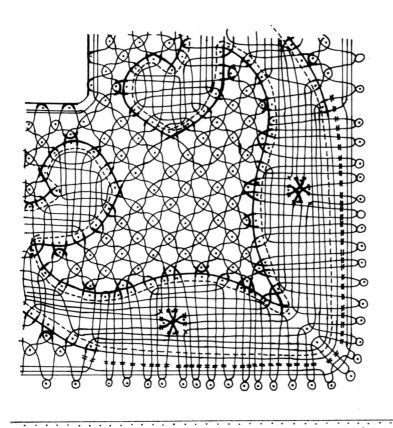

DIAGRAM 53.

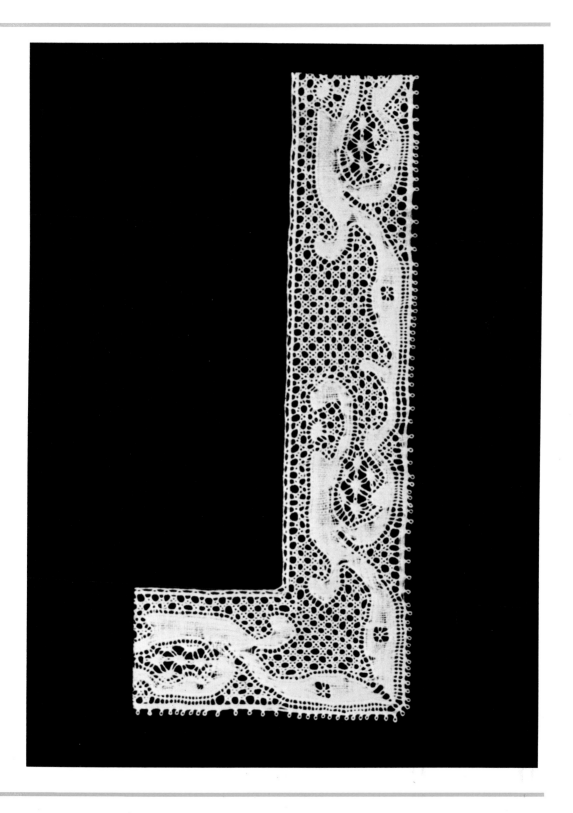

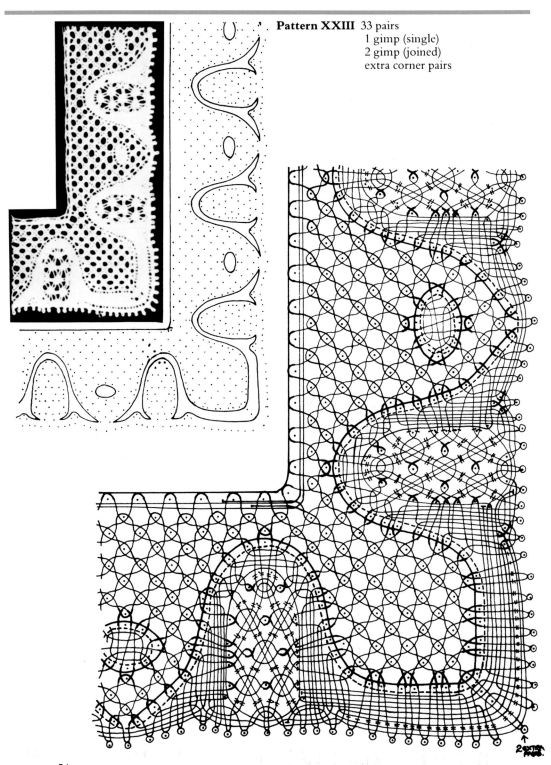

Pattern XXIII 33 pairs
1 gimp (single)
2 gimp (joined)
extra corner pairs

DIAGRAM 54.

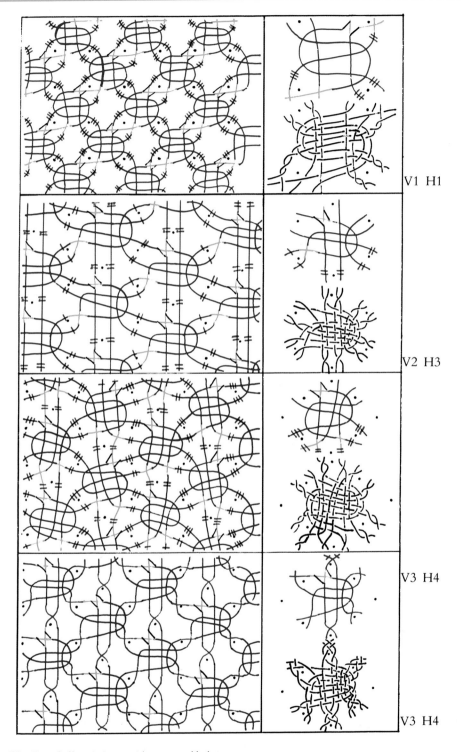

V1 H1

V2 H3

V3 H4

V3 H4

DIAGRAM 55. *Snowball variations, without central holes*

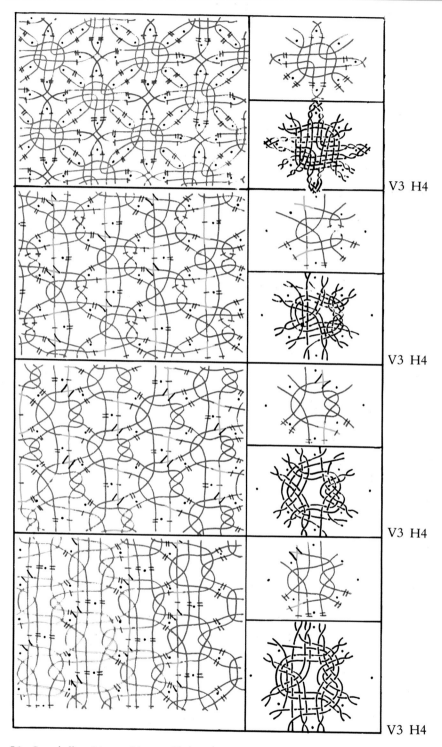

V3 H4

V3 H4

V3 H4

V3 H4

DIAGRAM 56. *Snowball varitions, with central hole*

Pattern XXIV 26 pairs

This pattern is similar to that called 'The little stones', which is occasionally found amongst laces made during the 1920s and 1930s, being popular for handkerchief and 'modesty' edgings. In the pattern here a snowball filling has been used instead of the more usual large snowflake. The pattern has also been adapted to include a straight-line beginning and finishing of a cloth stitch area

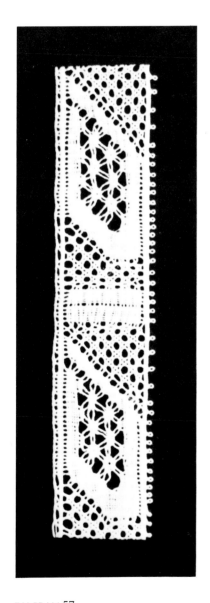

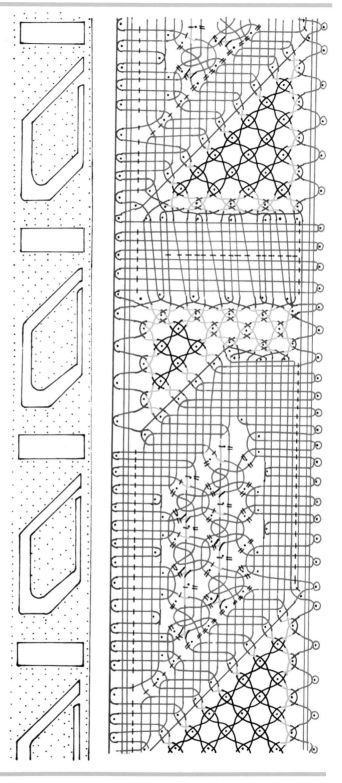

DIAGRAM 57.

10

More advanced patterns

Special shapes and movement of threads. Old techniques.

The patterns in this chapter include many of the older techniques mentioned in the historical notes of earlier chapters. In some patterns the movement of the threads makes the use of a gimp thread unnecessary; at the same time this requires greater sensitivity and care in the handling of the tension of the threads, so that the cloth stitch areas may remain as even as possible.

Fig. 1. Pattern XXV 31 pairs (joined in pairs)
4 pairs (single) to add
2 gimp (joined)

In this pattern the pairs are hung on pins to start with a double picot

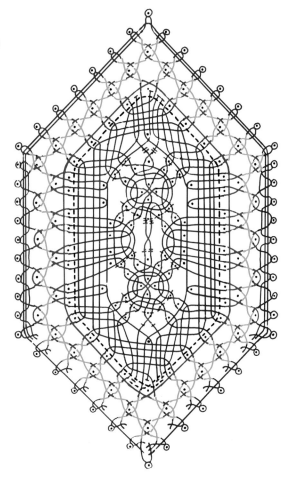

Fig. 2. The method of starting from a pin with a double picot

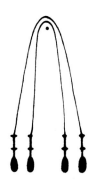 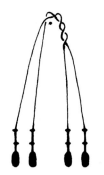 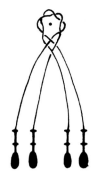 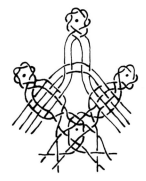

DIAGRAM 58.

89

Fig. 1. Finishing off pairs on an
angled picoted edge

*Pairs once worked back across the edging cloth stitch to
finish are placed to the back of the pillow. These threads
are cut after the lace has been finished, but whilst still on
the pillow. At point A be sure to leave all threads long
enough in order that they may be sewn through the
backing cloth when the lace is mounted. Do all final
trimming when the lace is off the pillow and all bobbins
have been removed*

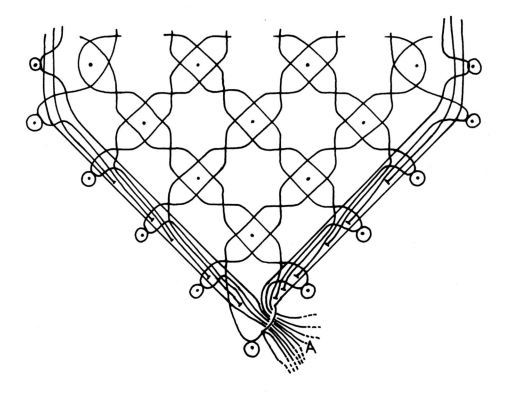

DIAGRAM 59.

Fig. 2. Pattern XXVI 31 pairs (joined in pairs)
1 pair (joined) for later addition

Note the difference in the picot edging techniques in
patterns XXV and XXVI

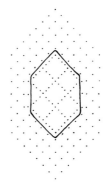

Pattern XXVII 25 pairs plus one extra for the corner
This pattern has been developed from a small part of a seventeenth-century Antwerp lace.

DIAGRAM 60.

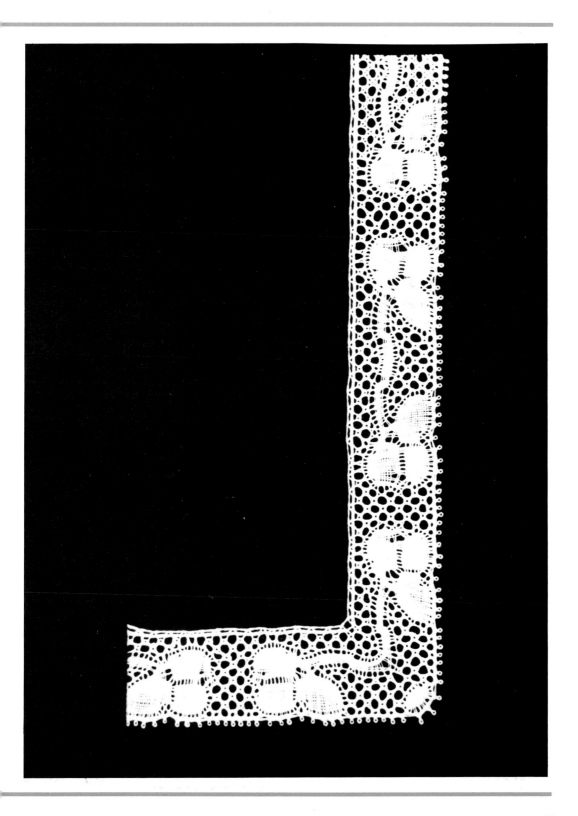

Pattern XXVIII. *This pattern was developed from a small part of an early eighteenth-century Antwerp lace.*

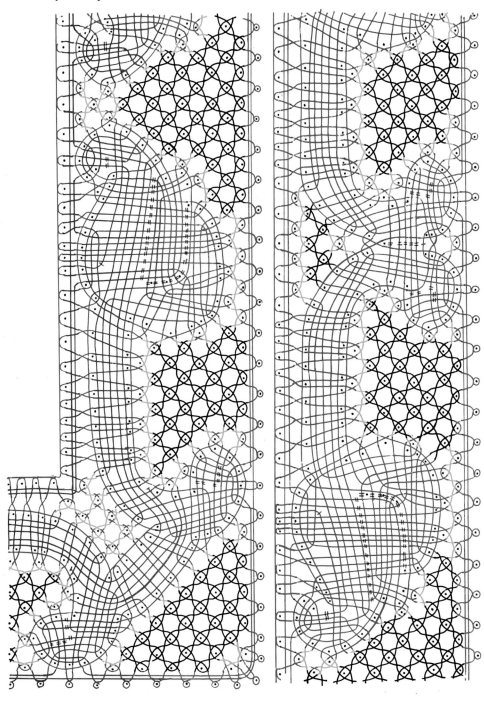

DIAGRAM 61.

Pattern XXVIII 29 pairs, plus one
extra for the corner.
See diagram 61 for the working diagram.

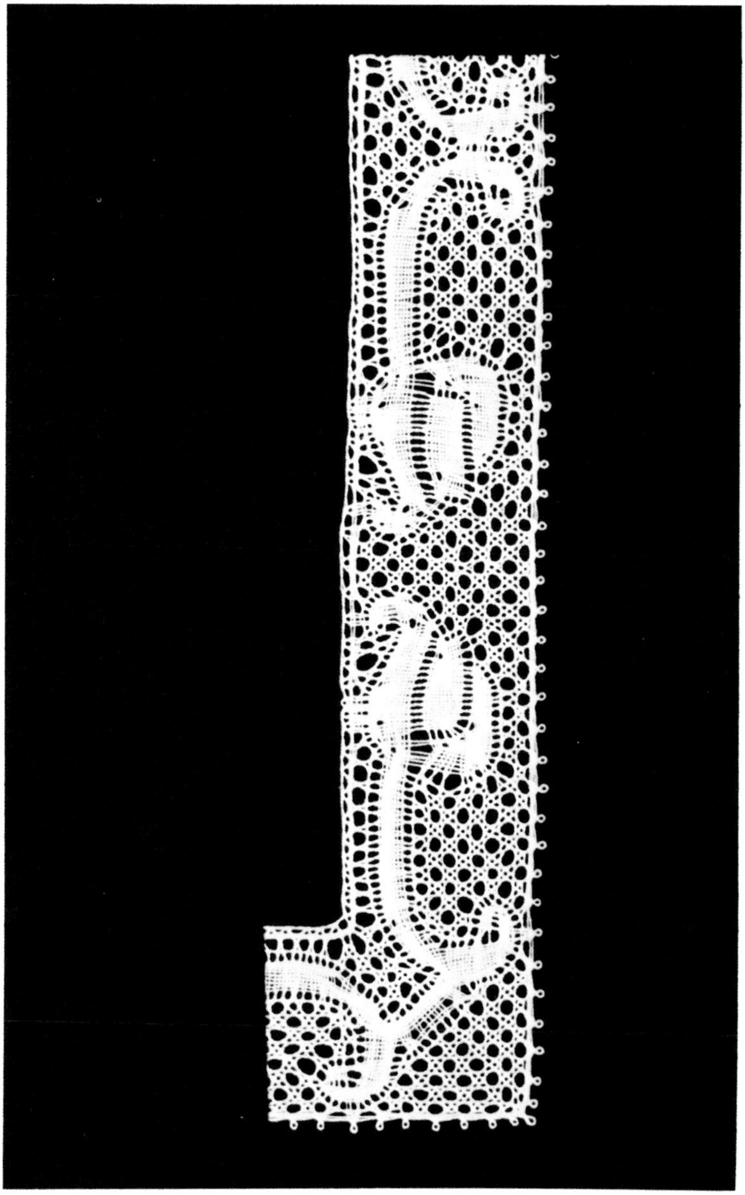

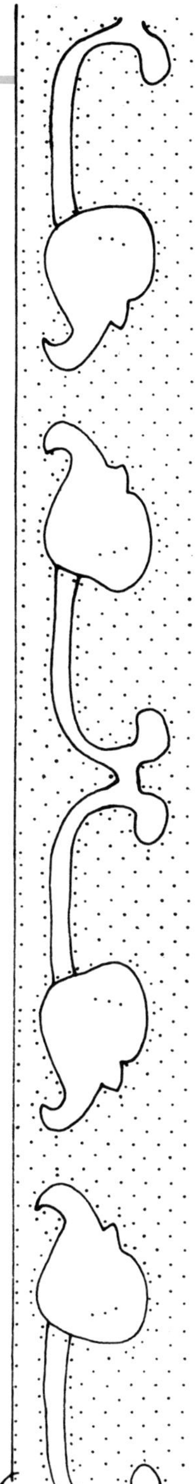

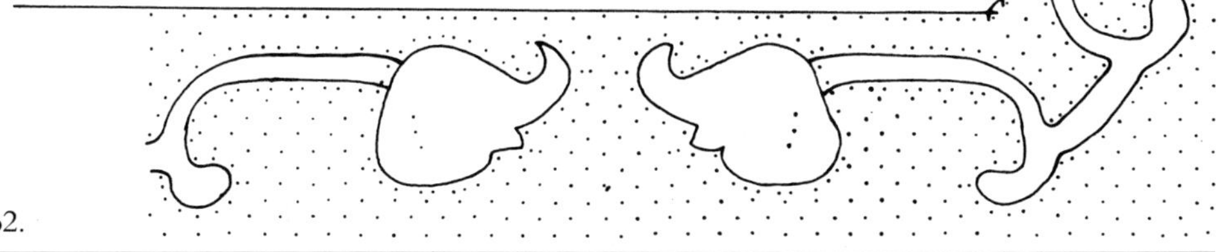

DIAGRAM 62.

Pattern XXIX. 56 pairs to start
3 pairs (unjoined for cat's body)
(*See diagram 64 for working diagram*)

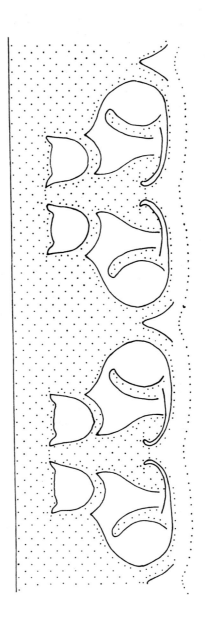

DIAGRAM 63.

Pattern XXIX. *Great care has to be taken with both the tensioning and securing of pairs with this pattern*

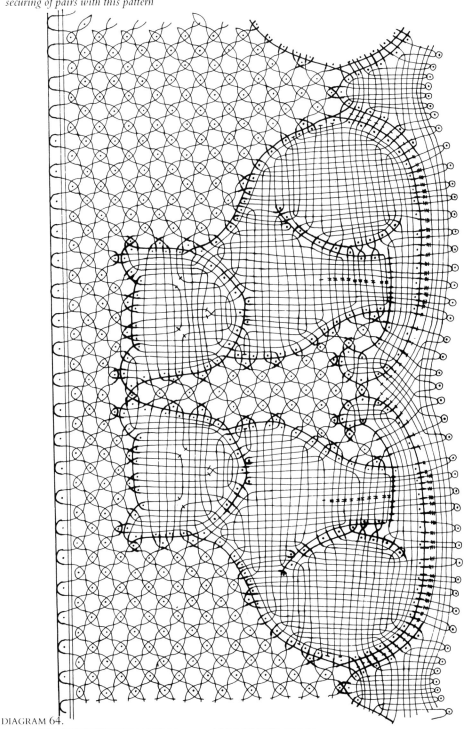

DIAGRAM 64.

Pattern XXX 44 pairs

This pattern has been adapted for bobbin lace from a piece made by a machine. Interestingly, this machine-made lace was most probably copied from an earlier bobbin-made piece of lace
(See diagram 66 for the working diagram)

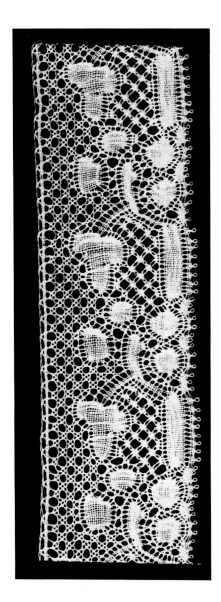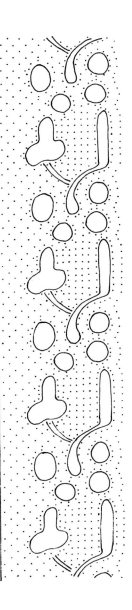

DIAGRAM 65.

Pattern XXX

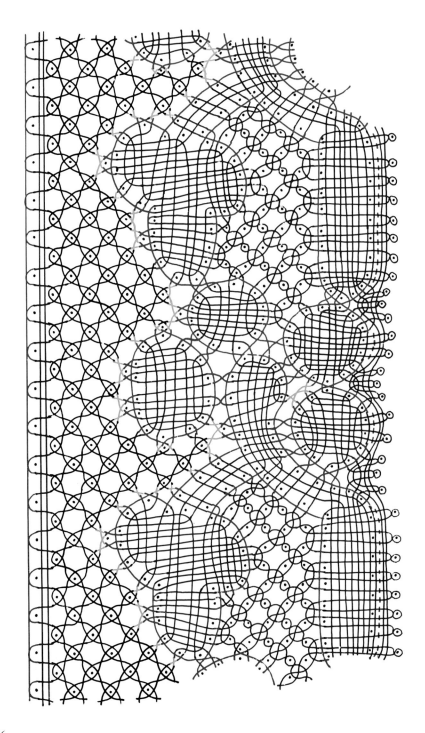

DIAGRAM 66.

99

Pattern XXXI 47 pairs
2 pairs extra for the corner

The basic motif to this pattern has been adapted from an early eighteenth-century Antwerp lace. Notice how the snowball fillings adapt to the varying number of pairs available. Care has to be taken in the handling of the tension of the pairs of threads moving through the larger areas of cloth stitch. (See diagram 68 for the corner working diagram)

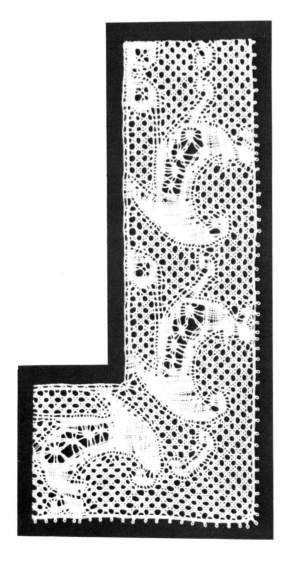

DIAGRAM 67.

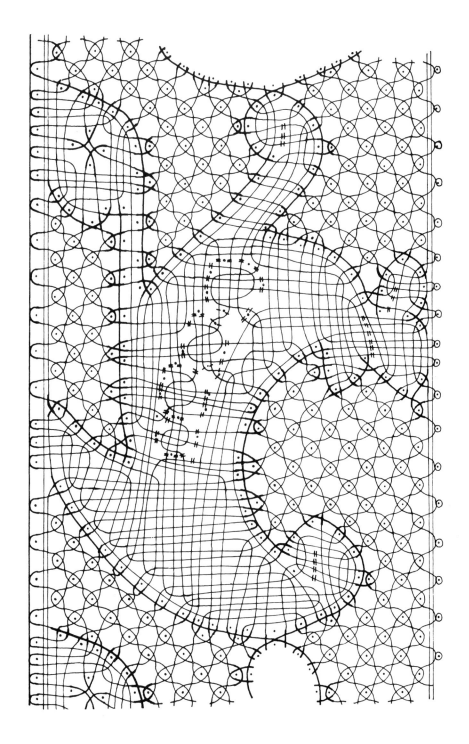

101

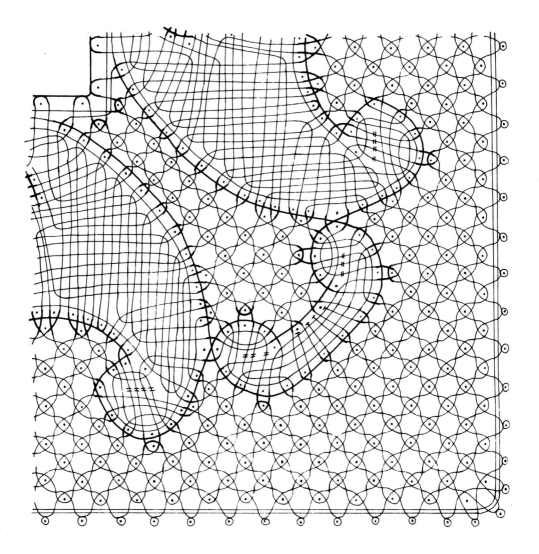

DIAGRAM 68.

Pattern XXXII

Based on the old Flanders techniques for creating linear shapes ending in small balls. This pattern contains a number of interesting thread movements. Great care has to be taken in certain areas with the tensioning of the threads (See diagram 70 for the working diagram)

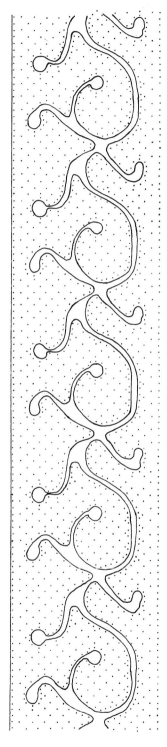

DIAGRAM 69

103

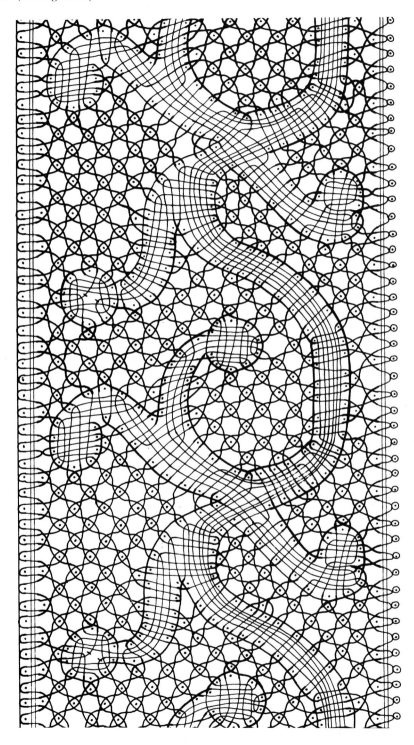

DIAGRAM 70.

Pattern XXXIV 48 pairs

DIAGRAM 71.

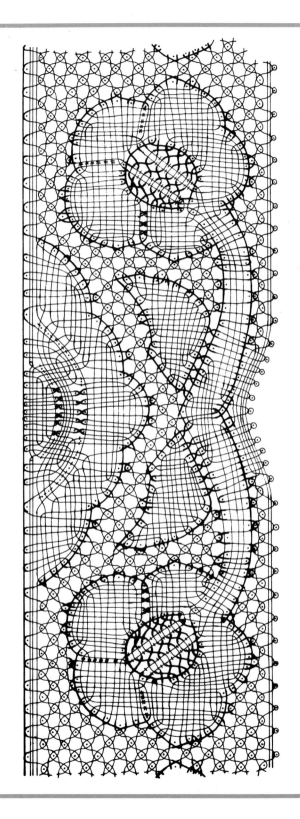

DIAGRAM 71. (*continued*)

Pattern XXXIV

This lace has been specially designed with a narrow footside in order that two matching pieces of lace could be joined together to make a single piece of lace suitable for a picture frame. The central filling to the flower is the same as that used in flower fillings of the early seventeenth century. Like the old filling this new one is also worked without pin supports

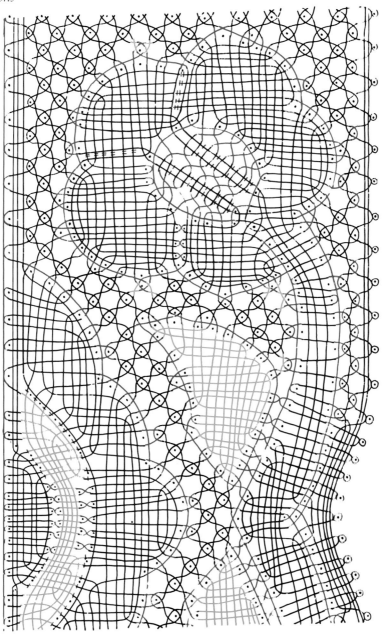

DIAGRAM 72.

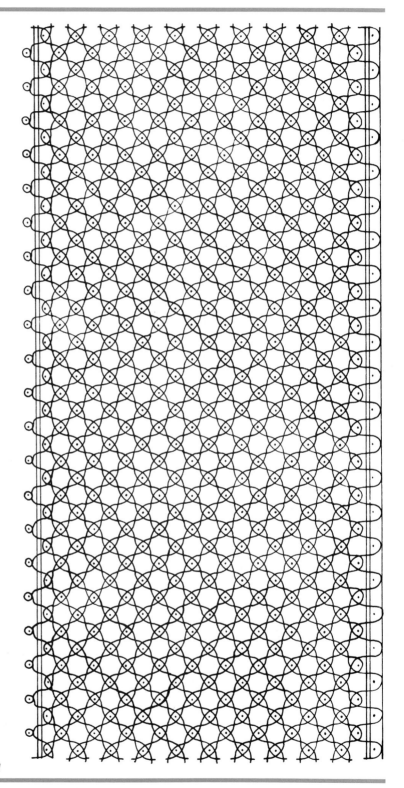

DIAGRAM 73. *Flanders ground*

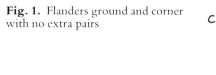

Fig. 1. Flanders ground and corner with no extra pairs

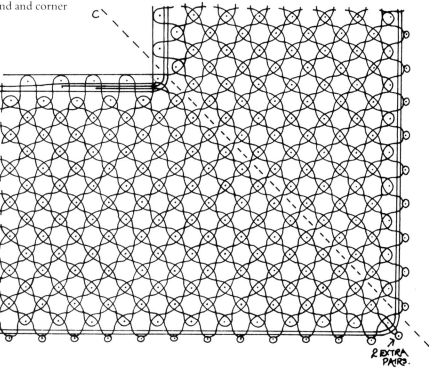

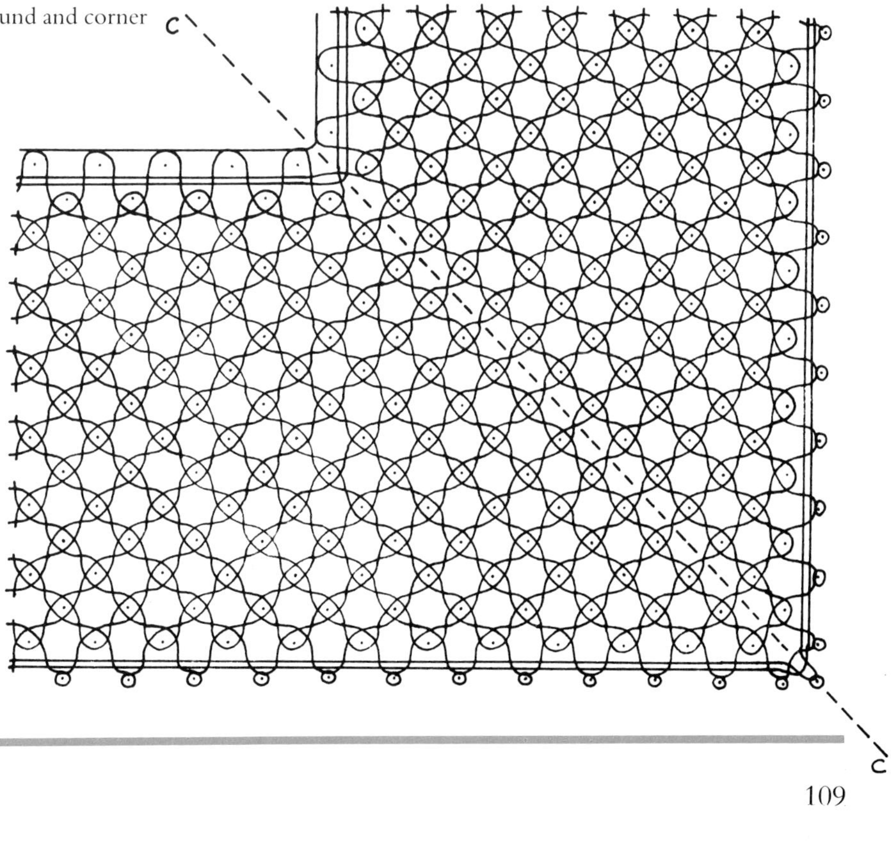

2 EXTRA PAIRS.

Fig. 2. Flanders ground and corner with two extra pairs

DIAGRAM 74.

Glossary

Aap Monkey, le singe, abe

Aanhaking Hooking-in, accrochage, sammenhækling

ærte Pea, bolleken, le pois

Antwerp Antwepen, Anvers

Anvers Antwep, Antwerpen

Bar Plait, bride, vlecht

Bobbin Klos, fuseau, kniplepin

Bolleken Pea motif, motif de pois, ærte

Bomuld Cotton, katoen, coton

Boule de neige Snowball, sneeuwbal, snebaal

Bourdon Gimp, sierdraad, fil de contour, indlægstraad

Brass pins Kopperen spelden, l'épingles en laiton, knappenaale

Bride Bar, plait, vlecht

Bund Ground, frond/trialie, réseau

Cane ground Five-hole ground, Flanders ground, Vlaandersetrialie, maille à cinq trous, cinqtrous bund

Chapeau de Curé Curate's hat, Pastershoedje, Præstens hat

Chopped straw Gehakt stro, crin végétal, hakket halm

Cloth stitch Linnenslag, toilé, lærreds slag

Cloth stitch and twist Gewrongen slag, passé tordues, dobbeltslag

Coin Corner, hoek, hjørne

Corner Hoek, coin, hjørne

Coussin Lace pillow, kussen, knipple pude

Coton Cotton, katoen, bomuld

Crin végétal Chopped straw, gehakt stro, hakket halm

Curate's hat Pasterhoedje, chapeau de Curé, Præstens hat

Cushion Lace pillow, kussen, coussin, knipple pude

Demi-passée Half stitch, halve slag, grillé, enkeltslag

Dobbeltslag Cloth stitch and twist, passée tordue

Draad Thread, fil, traad

Enkeltslag Half stitch, halve slag, demi-passée, grillé

Epingle (l') Pin, speld, knappenaale

L'épingle de support Support pin, Wegsteekspeld, stils

Fairy-point Toveresse kant, point de fée

Fil Thread, draad, traad

Fil de contour Gimp, sierdraad, bourdon, indlægstraad

Filling Vulling, fond, fyldning

Five-hole ground Cane ground, Flanders ground, Vlaanders grond, maille à cinq trous, cinqtrous bund

Flanders ground Cane ground, Vlaanders grond, maille à cinq-trous, cinqtrous bund

Fond Filling, vulling fyldning

Footside Zelfkant, lisière, sykant

Fuseau Bobbin, klossen, kniplepin

Fyldning Filling, vulling, fond

Gehakt stro Chopped straw, crin végétal, hakket halm

Gimp Sierdraad, bourdon, fil de contour, indlægstraad

Gewrongen slag Cloth stitch and twist, passée tordue, dobbeltslag

Grand point de neige Large snowflake, grote sneeuwvlok, stor snefnug

Grillé Half stitch, halve slaag, semi-passée, enkeltslag

Grote sneeuwvlok Large snowflake, grand point de neige, stor snefnug

Grond Ground, trialie, réseau, bund

Hakket halm Chopped straw, gehakt stro, crin végétal

Half stitch Halve slag, demi-passée, grille, enkeltslag

Halve slag Half stitch, demi-passée, grille, enkeltslag

Hjørne Corner, hoek, coin

Holes Open luchtje, trous, huller

Hooking-in Aanhaking, accrochage, sammenhækling

Hør Linen, linnen, lin

Horizontal Horizontaal, Vandret

Huller Hole, open luchtje, trous

Hul til knappenaal i prikkebrevet Pin-hole, speldegaatje, trous d'épingle

Indlægstraad Gimp, sieredraad, boudon, fil de contour

Kantenpaar Outlining pair, ring pair, pair de contour

Katoen Coton, coton, bomuld

Kleine sneeuwvlok Little snowflake, petit point de neige, lille snefnug

Kloefken Little clog, le petit sabot, lille Tæsko

Knappenaale Bobbin, klos, fuseau

Knipple pude Lace pillow, kussen, coussin

Kopperen spelden Brass pins, l'épingle en laiton, knappenaale

Kussen Lace pillow, coussin, knipple pude

Lace pillow Cushion, kussen, coussin, knipple pude

Lærreds slag Cloth stitch, linenslag, toilé

Lille snefnug Little snowflake, petit point de neige, Kleine sneeuwvlok

Lille tæsko Little clog, kloefken, le petit sabot

Linen Linnen, lin, hør

Linnenslag Cloth stitch, toilé, lærreds slag

Lisière Footside, zelfkant, sykant

Little clog Kloefken, le petit sabot, lille tæsko

Little snowflake Kleine sneeuwvlok, petit point de neige, lille snefnug

Lodret Vertical, vertikaal

Maille à cinq trous Cane ground, five-hole ground, Flanders ground, Vlaanderse trialie, cinqtrous bund

Malines Mechelen

Mechelen Malines

Monkey Aap, le singe, abe

Mønster Pattern, patroon, patron

Outlining pair Ring pair, kantenpaar, pair de contour

Pair de contour Outlining pair, ring pair, kanten paar

Pareltje Spangles, perles

Passement Plaited, fletted knipling

Passée tordue Cloth stitch and twist, gewrongen slag, dobbeltslag

Pastershoedje Curate's hat, chapeau de Curé, Præstens hat

Pattern Patroon, patron, mønster

Pea Bolleken, le pois, ærte

Perles Spangles, pareltje

Petit point de neige Little snowflake, kleine sneeuwvlok, lille snefnug

Picot Enkeloogje

Pillow Cushion, kussen, cousin, knipple pude

Pin Speldegaatje, trous d'épingle, hul til, knappenaal i prikkebrevet

Piqué Pricking, prikking, prikkebrev

Plait Bar, vlecht, bride

Point de fée Fairy point, toveresse kant

Pois (le) Pea, Bolleken, ærte

Præstens hat Priest's hat, Curate's hat, Pastershoedje, chapeau de Curé

Pricking Prikking, piqué, prikke brev

Prikke brev Pricking, prikking, piqué

Réseau Ground, grond/trialie, bund

Ring pair Outlining pair, kantenpaar, pair de contour

Sabot (le petit) Little clog, kloefken, lille tæsko

Sammenhækling Hooking-in, aanhaking, accrochage

Sea grass Zeegrass, crin végétal, sø græs

Sierdraad Gimp, bourdon, fil de contour, indlægstraad

Singe (le) Monkey, aap, abe

Sneball Snowball, sneeuwbal, boule de neige

Snoning twist, wringen, tordre

Snowball Sneeuwbal, boule de neige, snebaal

So græs Zeegras, crin végétal

Spangles Pareltje, perles

Speld Pin, l'épingle, knappenaal

Speldegaatje Pinhole, trous d'épingle, hul til knappenaal i prikkebrevet

Stils Support pin, wegsteekspeld, l'épingle de support

Stor snefnug Large snowflake, grote sneeuwvlok, grand point de neige

Support pin Wegsteekspeld, l'épingle de support, stils

Sykant Footside, zelfkant, lisière

Tæsko (lille) Little clog, kloefken, le petit sabot

Thread Draad, fil, traad

Toilé Cloth stitch, linnenslag, lærreds slag

Tordre Twist, wringen, snoning

Toveresse kant Fairy point, point de fée

Trialie Ground, ground, réseau, bund

Trous Hole, open luchtje, huller

Trous d'épingle Pinhole, speldegaatje, hul til knappenaal i prikkebrevet

Twist Tordre, snoning

Vandret Horizontal, horizintaal

Vertical Verikaal, lodret

Vlanderse trialie Cane ground, Flanders ground, maile à cinq trous, cinqtrous bund

Vlecht Bar, plait, bride

Vulling Filling, fond, fyldning

Wegsteekspeld Support pin, l'épingle de support, stils

Whole stitch Cloth stitch, linnenslag, toilé, lærreds slag

Working diagram Technische tekening, arbejdstegning

Wringen Twist, tordre, snoning

Zeegrass Sea grass, crin végétal, sø græs

Zelfkant Footside, lisière, sykant

Suppliers

Alby Lace Centre
Cromer Road
Alby
Norwich
Norfolk

Frank Herring & Sons
27 High West Street
Dorchester
DT1 1UP

Honiton Lace Shop
44 High Street
Honiton
Devon

D J Hornsby
149 High Street
Burton Latimer
Kettering
Northants

Capt J R Howell
19 Summerwood Lane
Halsall
Nr Ormskirk
Lancs L39 8RG

Sebalace
76 Main Street
Addingham
Ilkley
West Yorks
LS29 0PL

T Brown
Woodside
Greenlands Lane
Prestwood
Great Missenden
Bucks

A Sells
49 Pedley Lane
Clifton
Shefford
Beds

Enid Taylor Valley House Craft Studio
Ruston
Scarborough
North Yorks YO1 9QE

George White
Delaheys Cottage
Thistle Hill
Knaresborough
North Yorks, HG5 8LS

English Lace School
Honiton Court
Rockbeare
Nr Exeter
Devon

Mace and Nairn
89 Crane Street
Salisbury
Wilts

The Lace Guild
The Hollies
53 Audnam
Stourbridge
West Midlands

D H Shaw
47 Zamor Crescent
Thurscroft
Rotherham
South Yorks

John & Jennifer Ford
5 Squirrels Hollow
Boney Way
Walsall WS7 8YS

Shireburn Lace
Finkle Court
Finkle
Sherburn in Elmet
North Yorks

Newham Lace Equipment
15 Marlow Close
Basingstoke
Hants

B Phillips
Pantglas
Cellan
Lampeter
Dyfed

Mr Van de Weghe
Scharlaeken
Philipstockstraat 5-7
800 Brugge
Belgium

Tim Parker
10 Newcombe Road
Tuckton
Bournemouth
Dorset

Quality Belgian lace bobbins, large range:–

Marc de Maertelaere
Hooistraat 124
9210 Heusden
Belgium
(Wholesale and retail)

Index

Antwerp 28, 89, 92, 110

Binche 8, 9, 20, 27
bobbins 12-14, 110, 111
  adding pairs of 32, 38
  adjusting height of 12, 14
  removing pairs of 31, 32, 38

chevrons 43-7, 49, 50, 52, 58, 62, 63, 70-2, 79,
  80, 84, 92, 93, 96-9, 105-7
clogg, the 35, 111
colour coding system, Belgian 18, 19
corner 36-42, 110, 111
  double pointed 64-71
  motifs on 38, 42, 47-50, 52, 53, 62, 63, 65,
  68, 69, 79, 80, 82-4, 92-5, 100, 102
  moving lace for 36, 39, 40
cover cloth 12, 13, 40

fine-hole ground (Flanders ground) 8, 9, 20-3,
  25, 108-12
footside 21, 22, 26, 43, 44, 51, 54, 66, 67, 110,
  111, 112
  wavy edge 43, 44, 47, 48, 51-3, 68, 69

gimp 8, 15, 27, 30-2, 45, 56, 110, 111
grids 22, 23, 74, 75

holes 54, 55, 76, 77, 86, 96, 97, 103, 104, 111,
  112
hooking in 64, 66, 70, 72, 110, 111

lace
  to finish 24, 26, 90

joining 24, 26
  pillow 10, 11, 13, 110, 111
  stand for pillow 10, 11
  to start 23
l'oeil de perdrix 31, 32, 54, 55, 70, 71, 81, 83,
  100, 101

Mechelen 8, 9, 27, 111
monkey 54, 58-60, 110, 111

pea motif 27-31, 33, 34, 42, 49, 50, 62, 70, 71,
  79, 80-4, 98, 99, 110
  diagonal 28, 34
  large 31, 32
  round 28-30, 33, 34
picot
  edge 21-3, 26, 43, 44, 54
  to make 24
pins 15-17, 110-12
  support 15, 16

snowball 73, 74, 85-9, 91, 100, 101, 110, 112
snowflake
  large 73, 74, 76-81, 84, 112
  small 73-5, 78, 111
straight line beginning and finishing of cloth
  stitch areas 61, 62, 87, 96, 97

threads 14, 15, 110
  broken 12, 24, 26

Valencienne 27, 89

Grids used for lace pattern drafting

1. 5 mm squares

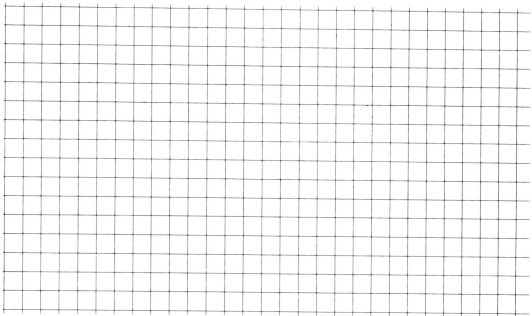

2. 6 squares = 25 mm (4 mm squares)

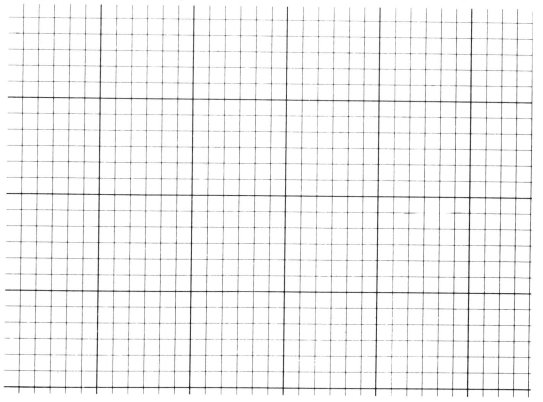

3. 8 squares = 25 mm (use 2 squares to give 4 sq. = 25 mm)

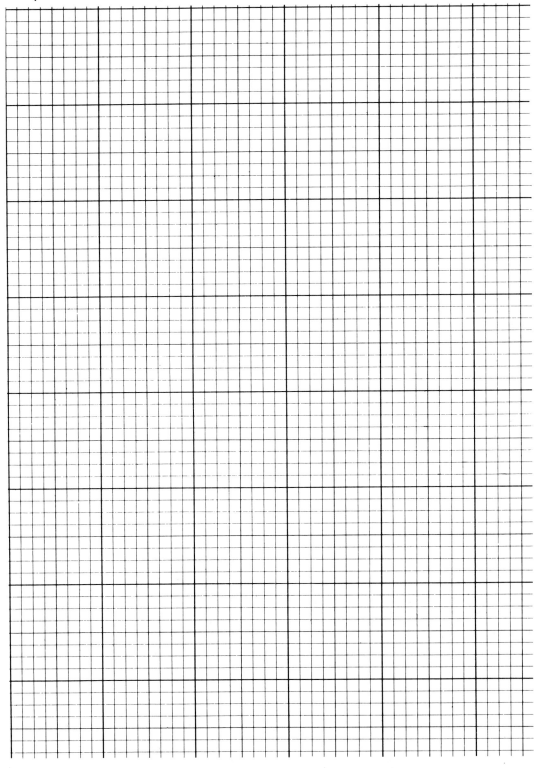

4. 10 squares = 25 mm

5. 2 mm squares

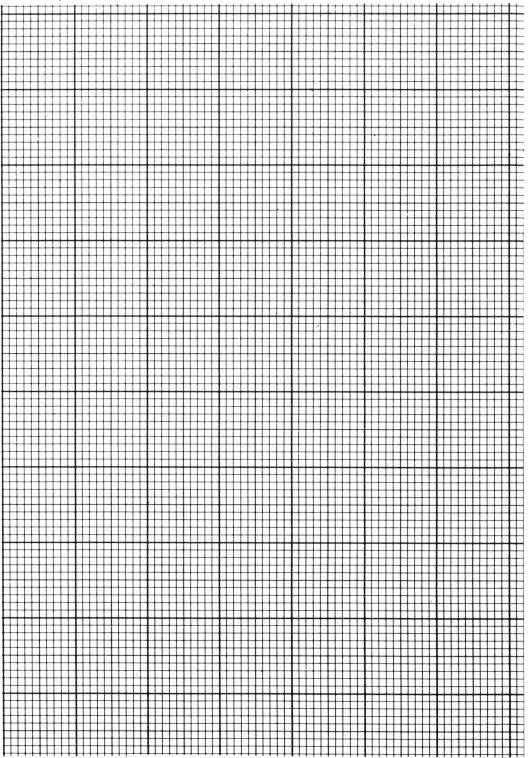